Architectures of the
Near Futu

G000092913

Architectural Design
September/October 2009

Guest-edited by Nic Clear

IN THIS ISSUE
Main Section

URBAN MYTH
Matthew Gandy, Professor of Geography at University College London, and Director of the UCL Urban Laboratory, questions the condition of city development in the 21st century. P 12

VISCERAL VISION
Bastian Glassner, of film directors Lynn Fox, simultaneously seduces and repels with his meaty and sumptuous images of fleshy fusion. P 30

SALIENT SATIRE
Ben Nicholson revisits his 2004 classic satire *The World Who Wants It?* and extends it to the current situation with fresh images and text. P 76

AD+

THE CULTURAL AFICIONADOS
Jayne Merkel profiles **Snøhetta** and describes how they have built their practice since their competition-winning Alexandria Library on the design of cultural centres. P 98+

CHEMICAL REACTION
Howard Watson visits **Hawkins\Brown's** new Biochemistry Department at Oxford University and finds a perfect assimilation of art, architecture and science. P 108+

WILEY
wiley.com

Architectural Design

Vol 79, No 5 (September/October 2009)
ISSN 0003-8504

Profile No 201
ISBN 978-0470 699553

Editorial Offices
John Wiley & Sons
International House
Ealing Broadway Centre
London W5 5DB

T: +44 (0)20 8326 3800

Editor
Helen Castle

Regular columnists: Valentina Croci, David Littlefield, Jayne Merkel, Will McLean, Neil Spiller, Michael Weinstock and Ken Yeang

Freelance Managing Editor
Caroline Ellerby

Production Editor
Elizabeth Gongde

Design and Prepress
Artmedia, London

Printed in Italy by Conti Tipocolor

Sponsorship/advertising
Faith Pidduck/Wayne Frost
T: +44 (0)1243 770254
E: fpidduck@wiley.co.uk

Front cover: Ben Marzys, *London After the Rain*, 2007. © Ben Marzys.

Subscribe to AD

AD is published bimonthly and is available to purchase on both a subscription basis and as individual volumes at the following prices.

PRICES
Individual copies: £22.99/$45.00
Mailing fees may apply

ANNUAL SUBSCRIPTION RATES
Student: UK£70/US$110 print only
Individual: UK £110/US$170 print only
Institutional: UK£180/US$335 print or online
Institutional: UK£198/US$369 combined print and online

Subscription Offices UK
John Wiley & Sons Ltd
Journals Administration Department
1 Oldlands Way, Bognor Regis
West Sussex, PO22 9SA
T: +44 (0)1243 843272
F: +44 (0)1243 843232
E: cs-journals@wiley.co.uk

[ISSN: 0003-8504]

Prices are for six issues and include postage and handling charges. Periodicals postage paid at Jamaica, NY 11431. Air freight and mailing in the USA by Publications Expediting Services Inc, 200 Meacham Avenue, Elmont, NY 11003.
Individual rate subscriptions must be paid by personal cheque or credit card. Individual rate subscriptions may not be resold or used as library copies.

All prices are subject to change without notice.

Postmaster
Send address changes to 3 Publications Expediting Services, 200 Meacham Avenue, Elmont, NY 11003

RIGHTS AND PERMISSIONS
Requests to the Publisher should be addressed to:
Permissions Department
John Wiley & Sons Ltd
The Atrium
Southern Gate
Chichester
West Sussex PO19 8SQ
England

F: +44 (0)1243 770620
E: permreq@wiley.co.uk

CONTENTS

Editorial

Helen Castle

The future is conventionally regarded as the bright light at the end of a tunnel. Untarnished and unfettered by the past and the present, it is populated by a better society, with increasingly ingenious gadgets and technologies all accommodated in shiny new buildings; as that well-known advertising adage goes: 'The Future is Orange'.

No discipline has been propelled forward more by the promise of the onward march of progress than architecture. Since the early 20th century, architects and designers have been smitten by the novel and the new. To this day, architecture as a discipline continues to judge itself on these terms, piling approbations on its star players that reflect this criteria: cutting-edge, avant-garde, innovative, experimental and ground-breaking. This is more about self-belief than client demand. Do those commissioning or using new buildings really believe that architects are constantly exceeding themselves?

What Nic Clear has so artfully realised through this issue of *AD* is that the act of projecting ourselves into the future can tell us more about the present than a literal reading of the current. As he states in his introduction, 'architectural projects can offer fantastic opportunities to develop narratives that can help us understand why we are doing the things we do'. This is particularly valuable in a period of uncertainty such as this when present commercial models of architectural practice have melted away along with the availability of credit for investment in construction and property, and a whole generation of young architects have found themselves stranded in a no-man's-land of recession. For the theme of the issue, Clear has reached outside architecture. He and many of his contributors have been inspired by science fiction in film and literature, and particularly by that of JG Ballard, who is illustrated on the page opposite by Clear.

The 'near' prefix of the title is as important to this issue as the word 'future' itself. It permits a certain degree of freedom in terms of interpretation, as it settles both on the very close and the not so close. This *AD* binds together extreme visions of dystopia – whether it is Bluewater Shopping Centre transformed into a sewer, or a shopping mall in Swindon eclipsed into a gout clinic – with articles that have their roots firmly in the gritty reality of the present day. This flexible, extendible lens enables a focus on the horrors and possibilities of the present. The contributors' words and images provide a poignant vision of the current that is as beautiful and disturbing as it is all too familiar. ⊿

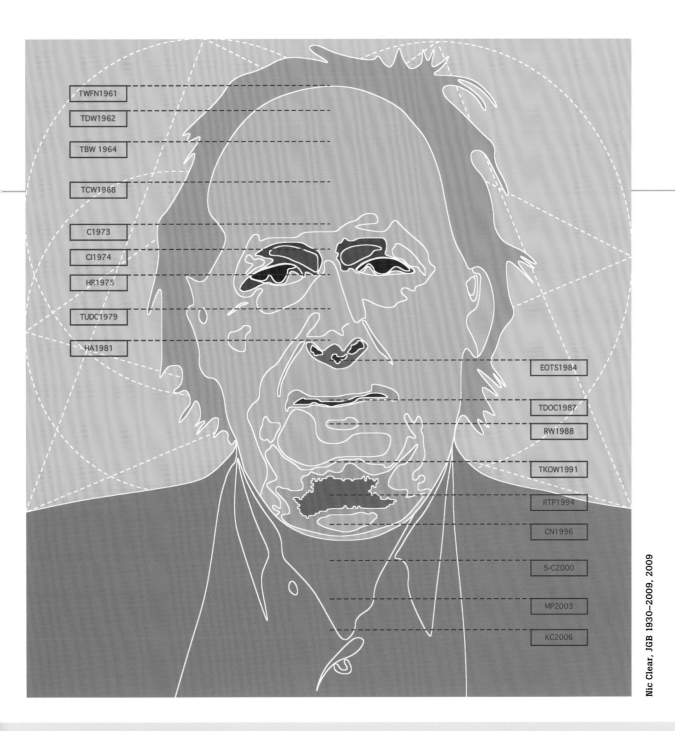

Nic Clear, JGB 1930–2009, 2009

JG Ballard, 1930–2009

James Graham Ballard was one of the most original and distinctive authors of the last part of the 20th century and the beginning of the 21st century. His writing encompassed topics as diverse as ecological crisis, technological fetishism, urban ruination and suburban mob culture, and he pursued these topics with a wit and inventiveness that is without equal.

Ballard's understanding of architecture and architects, and his prophetic visions, made him one of the most important figures in the literary articulation of architectural issues and concerns.

From the description of futuristic houses that empathise with their inhabitants, to the bleak characterisation of gated communities consumed by sex, drugs and violence, Ballard's world is highly prescient and ruthlessly unsentimental.

At a time when architectural discourse has become wholly subsumed by the moneymaking pre-occupations of the architectural profession, the writings of JG Ballard serve as reminder that architecture is about people, the things that they do and the places where they do them. Sometimes architecture will involve terrible people doing terrible things in terrible places, but the enduring nature of the human species is that we will always carry on; there is, after all, always the future.

Nic Clear, 2009

Introduction

A Near Future

By Nic Clear

Of all the arts, architecture is the closest constitutively to the economic, with which, in the form of commissions and land values, it has a virtually unmediated relationship.
Frederic Jameson, *Postmodernism, or, The Cultural Logic of Late Capitalism*, 1991, p 5[1]

Later, as he sat on the balcony eating the dog, Dr Robert Laing reflected on the unusual events that had taken place within this huge apartment building during the previous three months.
JG Ballard, *High Rise*, 1975, p 7[2]

Architectural design is always about the future; when architects make a proposition they always assume that it takes place in some imagined future. Architects nearly always assume that this future will be 'better' than the present, often as a consequence of what is being proposed. Architecture is, by its very nature, utopian.

Contemporary architecture, unlike earlier models of 'utopian' architecture, or perhaps because of the stigma attached to those models, has resisted an explicitly social and political agenda. Instead it has become driven by 'ideal' formalist agendas facilitated by the 'shape-making' potential of new computer-based design tools and funded by speculative finance.

Indeed, the most important transformations that have occurred in architecture over the last 30 years have not been in the shifts in fashion marking out new typologies, new forms of representation, new materials or new forms of manufacture; the biggest single shift has been in the new economic relations within the building industry and the new forms of contractual relationships that this has brought about. The rise of fast-track construction in the 1980s heralded a major change in the motivations for construction and brought about a homogenisation of building output largely predicated on maximising the economic value of the project, often with little regard for its social value.

And with the introduction of the Private Finance Initiative (PFI) the current UK government has turned even health-care and educational building programmes into a speculative enterprise. PFI has always been presented as a cost-effective way of financing large infrastructural projects; however, like the government's recent bail out of the banks, it works on the principle of the public financing the risk while the private sector skims off the profit.[3]

For a number of years the single model that has shaped the type of future that the architectural profession has based its assumptions on is one of unfettered consumer expansion. The majority of recent architectural debates have not tried to call into question the economic imperatives of late capitalism that drive financial speculation and generate the context within which private development is presented as the only option. Even the avant-garde architectural firms of the 1980s are now operating as large international commercial practices, and the Deconstructivists have proved to be more than enthusiastic capitalists. The critical and intellectual ambitions inspired by Jacques Derrida, Gilles Deleuze and Guy Debord have been replaced with the monetarist ideologies of Milton Friedman and Alan Greenspan.

The architectural profession has embraced the late capitalist model enthusiastically and uncritically, while all the time pandering to the concepts of social and environmental responsibility. The fact is that this model has been funded through speculative investment, and now that the money has run out the profession is bereft of alternatives.

The promise of an 'urban renaissance' has left buildings empty and negative equity is becoming once again the dominant economic value across the property world.

The architectural world has proved completely incapable of suggesting what the future may hold; can one still believe in the shiny renders of the corporate architectural complex when this world has replaced a vision of the future with an image of the future?

But the profession is resourceful and in the same way that all contemporary architects play the 'sustainability' game, whether they are designing sustainable airports, sustainable shopping centres, sustainable luxury hotels, sustainable office blocks, sustainable cities in the middle of deserts or sustainable single private dwellings for the ultrarich, we will, no doubt, see a gritty 'new realism' starting to appear in architectural discourse that responds to the new economic conditions.[4]

Exactly how these new imperatives will drive the formal shape-making methodologies that have filled so many glossy pages for so long we shall see; and how will the interactive and responsive landscapes interact with, and respond to, bankruptcy, increasing unemployment and a general sense of despair?

Nic Clear, Game with Vestiges:
After Ballard Triptych, 2009
The series of drawings here was
set up in the same way as any
standard CAD drawing in
VectorWorks using layers,
classes and libraries of objects.
The drawings work as a
narrative triptych, bringing
together a number of elements –
cityscapes, high-rise buildings,
surrealist curios, fetish and banal
objects – all in keeping with the
memory of 'Jim', to whom the
drawings are dedicated.

Progress

Contemporary culture has put its faith in the ideology of progress; progress will make things better, as well as making things faster and smaller (or bigger depending on the value system). This faith in progress and betterment fails to ring true in the light of economic downturn, environmental catastrophe, increased levels of crime, the threats of terrorism and global pandemics.[5] If the future cannot be guaranteed, where does that leave architecture?

However, a loss of faith is only a problem if that faith exists in the first place.

Within literature there is a major strand that looks at the future in a completely different way; science fiction can also be seen as a 'utopian' genre,[6] and in works by writers ranging from Jules Verne and HG Wells, through to Aldous Huxley and George Orwell and more latterly Philip K Dick, JG Ballard, Neal Stephenson and William Gibson, the future is depicted in a variety of different hues, not all of them as rosy as the futures promised by the architectural profession. As a result such speculations are often more believable.

While these writings appear to reflect on the future, more often than not they are actually concerned with issues contemporaneous to their production. To cite two obvious examples, Huxley's *Brave New World* (1932) and Orwell's *1984* (1949) are political reflections on the societies around them, and in Huxley's case it is not altogether clear whether he is entirely critical of the world that he describes.

However, the writings of JG Ballard are of particular interest here as they filter through a number of the texts contained in this issue, either directly or lingering in the background.[7] Ballard is of special significance largely due to the fact that in so much of his writing architecture and architects play such a pivotal role.

The prescience of Ballard's writing is obvious; his early works encompass environmental disaster, both drought and flooding; in the 1970s, novels such as *Crash*[8] and *High Rise*[9] dealt with technological fetishisation, urban anomie and alienation, and, long before such issues hit the mainstream, he looked at the links between consumerism and social collapse. In his recent writings, *Millennium People*[10] and *Kingdom Come*,[11] Ballard depicts a Britain bereft of social values other than those of daytime TV and the shopping centre, and while his central characters can lack credibility his general description of the cultural landscape is far more accurate than almost anything that has been published in the pages of any recent architectural publication.

The future as presented by Ballard is often stark, bleak and uncompromising. There are few happy endings in his future. However, his faith in our collective ability to endure almost any hardship, drawn almost certainly from his experiences in Shanghai during the Second World War, leads us to believe that despite whatever is thrown at us we will adapt and we will survive.[12]

Like Ballard, let us not despair; though the future may be uncertain, uncertainty is not without its attractions.

The current economic situation offers great potential for developing a new agenda in architecture. The fact that the discipline of architecture has become synonymous with the architectural profession is something that will no doubt become contested as unemployment rises throughout the building industry[13] – those of us who can remember previous recessions can also remember them as highly creative periods.

The fact that architects may have to redefine their operations is potentially a wonderful opportunity to recalibrate and reconsider who and what architecture is actually for.

This will bring to life the obvious gulf between expectation and reality that permeates architectural practice. Architecture is a wonderful discourse and training; however, it can be a very tedious job. Of course it does not have to be like this. Freed from the limitations of the profession, architectural projects can offer fantastic opportunities to develop narratives that can help us understand why we are doing the things we do.[14]

The fact that architects may have to redefine their operations is potentially a wonderful opportunity to recalibrate and reconsider who and what architecture is actually for.

In particular these uncertain times may be a blessing for a younger generation of designers; equipped with a vast array of technical skills and understanding they are almost certain to cope with the vagaries of future practice. As the skills demonstrated in many of the projects collected in this issue suggest, future architects may be just as adept at web design, graphics and film-making as they are at producing information for buildings.

The last few years have witnessed a gradual disenchantment within architectural education with the goals espoused by the architectural profession. Increased levels of student debt coupled with a creeping homogenisation of architectural practice have resulted in there being a darker aspect to student projects. Rather than shrinking away from the potential difficulties, the younger generation of architects may use information technologies to create new sites of architectural endeavour and give a whole new meaning to the term 'architectural design'.

The essays and projects gathered together here cover a wide variety of positions. Many develop the themes suggested by Ballard and others, while some give the current situation a broader historical perspective, suggesting that certain of the scenarios that we face are not without precedent.

Matthew Gandy's 'Urban Flux' gives a historical perspective to our current situation and argues that we need to recover the urban imagination in order to enrich 21st-century public culture. Michael Aling returns to his home town of Swindon, statistically the most average town in Britain, to find people sharing identities, stricken with gout and going to a deserted shopping centre for no real reason other than to fulfil a forgotten collective desire. And John Culmer Bell looks at the nature of electromagnetic radiation as a shaper of 19th- and 20th-century urban form, provocatively questioning whether sacrificing the pleasures of 'noctambulism' simply on environmental grounds is actually a good thing.

Bastian Glassner of *uber*-trendy video directors Lynn Fox presents a series of luxurious images, hybridising the body as meat, a clear homage to Francis Bacon (pun intended) with a bit of Roland Barthes' *A Lover's Discourse* thrown in.

Soki So reimagines Piranesi's *Carceri* as a near-future Hong Kong with a series of appropriately spectacular and sumptuous images that also address real concerns over the concept of urban intensity and vertical sprawl. Rubedo send out a provocative declaration concerning the omnipresence of technological systems and the necessity of developing transdisciplinary tactics to negotiate the immersive hybridised spaces of late capitalism.

Richard Bevan constructs a worryingly believable scenario whereby Heathrow airport becomes a carbon casino trading in carbon credits with air-mile-hungry oligarchs gambling to stay aloft, and Geoff Manaugh explores and questions the use of the term 'feral city'. In 'London After the Rain', Ben Marzys presents a beautiful graphic Surrealist landscape, a posthuman picturesque. In 'L.A.W.u.N Project #21: Cybucolia' the Invisible University suggest that the near future may carry with it many of the seeds sown with 19th-century Romanticism; and Dan Farmer suggests that the near future may be all in the mind with excerpts from his research on cortical plasticity. Ben Nicholson reflects on his 2004 book *The World Who Wants It?*, one of the finest pieces of satirical writing of recent years, and presents a series of images that were absent from the original publication.

Simon Sellars and George Thomson explore the most explicitly Ballardian line, with Sellars looking at the aural nature of the urban environment, beautifully illustrated with Michelle Lord's exquisite assemblages, and Thomson reimagining Ballard's 'Sound-Sweep' as a community occupying a derelict M25.

Finally, Art in Ruins show work from installations that are 20 years old, an important conceptual reminder that none of the ideas in this issue are particularly new.

This issue was first conceived in 2007; the proposal was put forward in early 2008 and most of the text written late 2008/early 2009. You will be reading this, at the very earliest, in autumn 2009. Like any other architectural project its relevance is shaped by a number of external forces far beyond the control of its authors; the economic events that are taking place as this text is being written (and rewritten) make any allusion to future certainties look foolish. The severity of the current economic situation makes any attempt to try to predict what light, if any, is at the end of this particular tunnel seem absurd. However, what happens if we imagine a number of scenarios, not necessarily the usual convivial scenarios that mainstream architecture usually relies on, but scenarios where the traditional certainties are replaced by something less predictable? Like the heroes of many of Ballard's stories, the authors of the essays in this issue face the future with a sense of resigned stoicism and the ability to create beauty wherever they find it.

In many ways the near future could be very much like the past, with one obvious exception – it will be completely different. ∆

Notes
1. Frederic Jameson, *Postmodernism, or, The Cultural Logic of Late Capitalism*, Duke University Press (Durham, NC), 1991, p 5.
2. JG Ballard, *High Rise*, Jonathan Cape (London), 1975, p 7.
3. See George Monbiot, 'The Biggest Weirdest Rip Off Yet', *Guardian*, 7 April 2009. In this article, Monbiot references a paper published in 2002 in the *British Medical Journal* in which five key criticisms were made of the PFI funding of hospitals: 1) that PFI brings no new capital investments; 2) that the assessments of value for money are skewed in favour of private finance; 3) the higher costs of PFI are due to financing costs which would be incurred under public financing; 4) any PFI schemes only show value for money after 'risk transfer', for risks that are not justified; 5) PFI more than doubles the cost of capital as a percentage of annual operating income. From Allyson M Pollock, Jean Shaoul and Neil Vickers, 'Private finance and "value for money" in NHS hospitals: a policy in search of a rationale?', *BMJ*, Vol 324, 18 May 2002, pp 1205–09.
4. One can imagine that such texts have already begun to emanate from Rotterdam and Boston.
5. For a critique of 'progress', see John Gray, *Heresies Against Progress and Other Illusions*, Granta Books (London), 2004.
6. See Frederic Jameson, *Archaeologies of the Future: The Desire Called Utopia and Other Science Fictions*, Verso (London and New York), 2005.
7. Ballard has been a central interest of my diploma unit at the Bartlett School of Architecture where I have been running a programme entitled 'Architecture of the Near Future' for several years. The work of Michael Aling, Richard Bevan, Dan Farmer, Ben Marzys, Soki So and George Thomson, all contributors to this issue, came out of this programme.
8. JG Ballard, *Crash*, Jonathan Cape (London), 1973.
9. JG Ballard, *High Rise*, op cit.
10. JG Ballard, *Millennium People*, Flamingo (London), 2003.
11. JG Ballard, *Kingdom Come*, Fourth Estate (London), 2006.
12. Beautifully described in his memoir *Miracles of Life: Shanghai to Shepperton*, Fourth Estate (London), 2008.
13. Job losses in architecture between February 2008 and February 2009 were reportedly up by 760%. See Will Hirst, 'Architect Job Losses up by 760%', *Building Design*, 20 March 2009, p 3.
14. The drawings that accompany this essay come from my sheer enjoyment of producing CAD drawings simply because they are something I like doing.

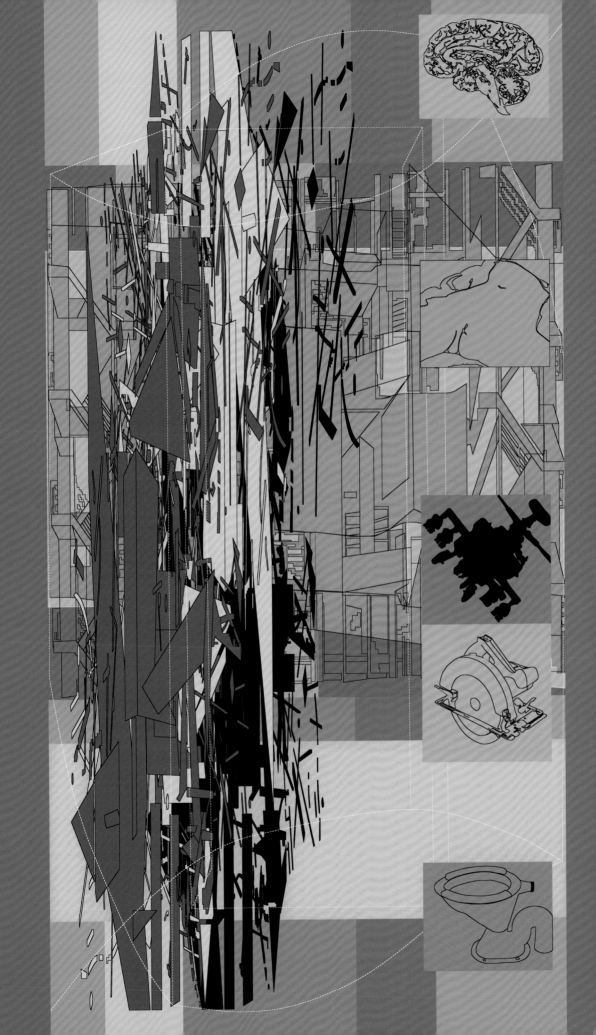

Urban

Flux

In the 21st century, why does the type of poverty and human exploitation most readily associated with Dickensian London or the 'dark Satanic Mills' of Victorian England still persist today? **Matthew Gandy**, Professor of Geography at University College London, and Director of the UCL Urban Laboratory, lifts the lid on the unevenness of global development, revealing why contemporary urban space continues to be characterised by landscapes of neglect interspersed with areas of intense investment and consumption.

In the early hours of 26 August 2005 a fire swept through a dilapidated apartment in central Paris crowded with African immigrants. Among 17 dead there were 14 children. In April 2005 another similar fire had killed 24 people, again mostly poor immigrants. The buildings in which these people lived were unfit for human habitation: cracked walls, lead paint, dangerous wiring, infested with vermin. In 2004 some 100,000 people were searching for social housing in Paris, a marked increase on 10 years earlier, but only 12,000 homes were allocated, leading to excessive overcrowding.[1]

In Paris and other ostensibly prosperous cities we find the persistence of 19th-century forms of poverty and human exploitation. In some cases, the very same areas, such as London's Somers Town or Manchester's Ancoats, have remained centres of deprivation for centuries. In the cities of the global South the scale of suffering and human degradation is far worse, yet the technical means to improve urban living conditions are not obscure – better housing, improved health care, modern plumbing and so on. Despite the efforts of early social scientists to demonstrate the connections between labour markets and poverty, or the role of public health advocates in forcing improvements in the way cities are managed, we have nonetheless retained nefarious elements of the 19th-century city ranging from inept forms of urban governance to renewed moral admonitions towards the poor.

The characteristic urban form associated with the modern city masks a diversity of different elements. In a colonial or postcolonial context we find that these 'multiple modernities' are even more apparent through the interweaving of different geometries of power, belief and social stratification. The relationship between democracy and the public realm, for example, is scarcely addressed in the recent elision between neo-liberal reform and the imposition of 'good governance' that has characterised much recent writing on policy dilemmas facing the cities of the global South.[2] Yet the weakness of the state, particularly beyond middle-class enclaves, necessitates an expanded definition of power to account for the daily practices through which resources such as land, water and shelter rights are actually allocated. The urbanisation of nature and the concomitant development of elaborate technological networks have involved an intersection between established sources of state authority and a plethora of other actors. Cities of the global South have been

Oshodi, Lagos, 2003
Market spaces are the fulcrum of the urban economy but are also potential sites for social and ethnic violence.

simultaneously shaped by officially acknowledged forms of state intervention in combination with an expanding zone of local negotiations to produce a 'shadow state' where the boundaries between different loci of political authority and legitimacy become extensively blurred.[3]

It is striking how fear and disdain for the urban poor remains so powerful today through the proliferation of gated communities and the clearing away of informal settlements. In India, for example, the war on the poor has become one of the dominant elements of environmental demands to 'clean up' cities and remove 'encroachers and polluters'.[4] Whether in London or Mumbai, a vast army of cheap labour is needed to allow the urban economy to function, yet the rich increasingly prefer not to mix with these people. Many architects and planners acquiesce in these processes, seemingly willing to transform cities into playgrounds for the wealthy where professional ethics is subsumed by the cult of celebrity, real-estate speculation and a new homogeneity in urban life.[5]

The landscape of the modern city bears the imprint of successive cycles of investment in the built environment: new waves of construction leave their mark through characteristic architectural styles or morphological arrangements of different elements.

The landscape of the modern city bears the imprint of successive cycles of investment in the built environment: new waves of construction leave their mark through characteristic architectural styles or morphological arrangements of different elements. In London, for example, significant tracts of Bloomsbury and Mayfair are the outcome of Georgian speculation while the expansion of railways in the Victorian era fuelled the growth of new suburbs such as Clapham and Wandsworth. Similarly, in the 20th century, the building of the London underground fostered waves of development in proximity to stations on the urban fringe, most notably 'Metroland' along the newly extended Metropolitan Line.

The ebb and flow of capital investment in urban space has produced a complex layering of forms and structures so that remnants of past waves of economic prosperity, such as empty factories or workshops, are either obliterated to make way for new developments or converted into new uses such as shopping malls or luxury housing. Early experiments in the reuse of former industrial spaces in Baltimore, London and other cities now extend to centres of transnational consumption at a global scale: the former mills of Mumbai's Lower Parel district, for example, are being busily converted into galleries, shops and luxury apartments.

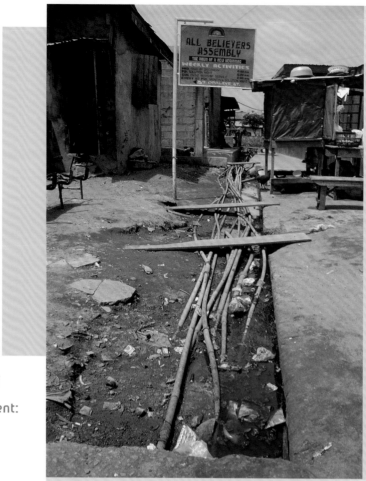

Amukoko, Lagos, 2003
A tangled mass of water pipes passing through an open sewer in a city where religiosity has increasingly supplanted political discourse.

In tandem with the transformation of the visible city we find that an invisible city of urban technological networks – largely hidden from view beneath the city streets – has also undergone profound changes. Successive waves of technology have produced a complex mass of pipes and wires to produce a physical mesh that is now juxtaposed with the emerging wireless city to produce an increasingly differentiated patchwork of connectivity in comparison with the more standardised landscapes associated with the Fordist metropolis.

Since the middle decades of the 19th century we find a periodicity in levels and patterns of investment in the physical infrastructure of cities that is reflective of prevailing macro-economic conditions and the changing institutional context for banking and finance. In addition to longer-term economic waves associated with technological innovations – so-called Kondratieff waves – economic historians have identified smaller cycles associated with particular forms of investment such as real estate, raw materials or agriculture. Though the explanations for these fluctuations explored by Schumpeter, Kuznets and others have now been subject to extensive critique, there nonetheless remains extensive empirical evidence for distinct 'building cycles' in relation to the development of cities that lead to instability in housing markets, construction activity and other key

Carson, Los Angeles, 2002
Looking south, a vast and largely deserted landscape
of pylons next to the Los Angeles River.

elements underpinning capitalist urbanisation.[6] In
periodic episodes of economic turbulence we can
encounter sudden and dramatic devaluation of existing
components of capital stock so that even recently
completed office or retail spaces may in some instances
be simply abandoned: the Asian financial crisis of
1995–7, for example, was partly driven by an over-
investment in real-estate profits that depended on the
stability of local currencies.[7]

The implications of the current global crisis have yet to
be fully manifested as the effects of the banking and
mortgage crisis begin to work their way through
successive national economies. These 'switching crises'
are enabled by the mobility of capital and its incessant
search for higher rates of return: a short-term ruthlessness
that is being underpinned by the growing power of
institutional shareholders such as pension funds.[8]

Contemporary urban space is characterised by
landscapes of neglect interspersed with intense foci of
capital accumulation and elite consumption: in the case
of London, for example, earlier waves of gentrification

have been superseded by new patterns of consumption that are
transnational in their orientation.[9] Vast managerial remuneration
packages on the back of inflated share values have distorted the entire
housing market leading to indebtedness for those on average incomes,
increased overcrowding and the rise of reactionary or neo-fascist
politics in working-class areas cut adrift from neo-liberal policy-
making. The growing market for exclusive properties has led to a spate
of new schemes such as a planned luxury housing project overlooking
Hyde Park in central London designed by Rogers Stirk Harbour +
Partners that includes penthouse flats to be offered at over £80
million. These flats – the most expensive ever constructed in the UK –
may feature bulletproof glass, specially purified air and 'panic rooms'
to protect against intruders.[10]

In the suburbs of Moscow or St Petersburg, mansions can be
commissioned on formerly publicly owned plots of land that exist as
digital projections under names such as 'Versaille' or 'English
Mansion'.[11] On the outskirts of Mumbai, a plethora of new elite
housing developments is under construction that draws readily on
pastoral imagery or aspects of ecological design such as Hiranandani
Gardens or Kalapataru Towers. Where land is not made readily
available to developers it can be acquired through corruption,

**Westin Bonaventure,
Los Angeles, 2002**
A symbol of
Postmodern theory and
architectural vacuity.

intimidation or indeed arson in the case of semi-arid coastal regions in the Mediterranean where protected areas have been destroyed to eliminate their biotic diversity and thwart possible planning restrictions. In more extreme cases land is forcibly released by vast slum clearances as in the neo-Hausmannite programme of urban regeneration currently under way in Indian cities such as Delhi or Mumbai, or the removal of poor communities through state-sponsored acts of mass violence, as in the anti-Muslim pogroms that recently swept through the centre of Ahmadabad.

The construction of luxury developments provides a lineage to authoritarian spaces of 'super consumption', such as Dubai, that are in turn linked to the geopolitical dynamics of organised crime, tax avoidance and oil wealth.[12] Property-led forms of urban regeneration are now operational in virtually all cities, even those such as Bologna, Copenhagen or Stockholm, which had previously sought to protect local housing markets from speculative pressures or had tolerated autonomous buildings or spaces on potentially valuable land.[13]

What alternatives exist for the 21st-century city? Certainly, we need to begin by disentangling past thinking: retain the 19th century's engineering brilliance, for example, but not its moral hypocrisy; nurture the 20th-century public realm, but not the autocratic or dysfunctional dimensions of state power. In the political sphere the idea of secular cosmopolitanism presents an alternative to the incessant drift towards greater division and segregation. Yet a cosmopolitanism that embraces cultural or ethnic difference is not to be confused with the pallid discourse of 'tolerance' where ignorance or suspicion is merely kept in abeyance.[14]

Intensifying global inequalities in wealth and poverty are marked by the vast growth of slums and the growing influence of transnational elites. Islands of gluttony also extend to the cities of the global north where spiralling income differentials, unstable housing markets and deteriorating public services are generating new landscapes of inequality and exclusion. The blocks of cramped, poor-quality housing that mark the 'regeneration' of London Docklands, for example, are a testament to London's denuded public realm and failure of imagination. Architects, planners and other professionals engaged in urban practice need to reflect on whether their projects are merely complicit elements in these processes or actively contributing towards a better future.

Alternative approaches to urban design are marked by a combination of long-term planning in the public interest and intricate engagement with clients to produce spaces that simultaneously fulfil a range of critical social,

cultural and environmental objectives. In the field of housing, for instance, we might look to the exemplary Sargfabrik in Vienna or Hegianwandweg in Zürich, which both combine innovative design with inclusive social agendas. Similarly, in terms of landscape, the Mile End Park in London and Petuel Park in Munich exemplify how marginalised or neglected spaces can be reintegrated within the city and enrich urban quality of life. In all these cases we encounter a longer-term urban vision that transcends speculative myopia: it is only by raising expectations that urban practice can meet the real needs of the contemporary city. ∆

Notes
1. David Fickling, 'Paris Apartment Fire Kills 17', *Guardian*, 26 August 2005.
2 Stuart Corbridge, Glyn Williams, Manoi Srivastava and Réne Véron (eds), *Seeing the State: Governance and Governmentality in India*, Cambridge University Press (Cambridge), 2005; Matthew Gandy, 'Planning, anti-planning and the infrastructure crisis facing metropolitan Lagos', *Urban Studies* 43(2), 2006, pp 71–96.
3. Barbara Harriss-White, *India Working: Essays on Society and Economy*, Cambridge University Press (Cambridge), 2003.
4. Partha Chatterjee, 'Are Indian cities becoming bourgeois at last?', in Indira Chandrasekhar and Peter C Seel (eds), *Body.city: siting contemporary culture in India*, Haus der Kulturen der Welt and Tulika Books (Berlin and Delhi), 2003, p 178.
5. Jonathan Raban, 'My Own Private Metropolis', *Financial Times*, 9–10 August 2008.
6. On the analysis of long waves in the capitalist economy see, for example, Angus Maddison, *Dynamic Forces in Capitalist Development: A Long-Run Comparative View*, Oxford University Press (Oxford), 1991; Ernest Mandel, *Late Capitalism*, trans Joris de Bres, Verso (London), 1977 [1972]; and Michael Marshall, *Long Waves of Regional Development*, Macmillan (London), 1987.
7. See, for example, Michael Pettis, *The Volatility Machine: Emerging Economies and the Threat of Financial Collapse*, Oxford University Press (Oxford), 2001; Joseph Stiglitz, 'Capital market liberalization, globalization and the IMF', *Oxford Review of Economic Policy* 20, 2004, pp 57–71. See also Ara Wilson, 'Bangkok, the bubble city', in Jane Schneider and Ida Susser (eds), *Wounded Cities: Destruction and Reconstruction in a Globalized World*, Berg (Oxford and New York), pp 203–26.
8. See, for example, Franklin R Edwards, 'Hedge funds and the collapse of long-term capital management', *The Journal of Economic Perspectives* 13, Spring 1999, pp 189–210. On the spatial dynamics of 'switching crises' in the capitalist economy see David Harvey, *The Limits to Capital*, Blackwell (Oxford), 1982. For recent developments within the global economy see Andrew Glyn, *Capitalism Unleashed: Finance, Globalization, and Welfare*, Oxford University Press (Oxford), 2006; David Harvey, *A Brief History of Neoliberalism*, Oxford University Press (Oxford), 2005.
9. Tim Butler and Loretta Lees, 'Super-gentrification in Barnsbury, London: globalization and gentrifying global elites at the neighbourhood level', *Transactions of the Institute of British Geographers* 31, 2006, pp 467–87.
10. '125-Millionen-Euro-Wohnung zu verkaufen'. *Welt online*, 5 March 2007.
11. Alex Veness, 'Capital disturbance', paper presented to the AHRC funded seminar 'In search of the urban pastoral', held at CABE (Commission for Architecture and the Built Environment), London, 29 March 2007. See also Tom Parfitt, 'Fear and Resentment as Moscow's Rich Grab Land for Luxury Homes', *Guardian*, 22 February 2007.
12. See Mike Davis, 'Fear and money in Dubai', *New Left Review* 41, 2006, pp 47–68.
13. In Stockholm, for example, gentrification pressures are occurring prior to transfers of tenure so that traditional explanations such as 'rent gap' theories need to be supplemented by a better understanding of the cultural dimensions to urban change and the influence of new urban elites. See Adam Millard-Ball, 'Moving beyond gentrification gaps: social change, tenure change and gap theories in Stockholm', *Urban Studies* 37, 2000, pp. 1673–93. See also M Franzén, 'New social movements and gentrification in Hamburg and Stockholm: a comparative study', *Journal of Housing and the Built Environment* 20, 2005, pp 51–77.
14. Vera Skvirskaya and Caroline Humphrey, 'Migration and the "post-cosmopolitan" city: The emergence of "tolerance" in Bukhara and Odessa," paper given at the Urban Salon, London, 10 March 2008.

POSTINDIVIDUALISM

FATA MORGANA AND THE

What might happen to Middle England if the retail and financial sectors were simply to melt away? Michael Aling casts a visionary eye on his home town of Swindon and imagines a dystopian future of 'post-individualism' in which retail mausoleums and gout clinics take the place of shopping malls and call centres.

SWINDON GOUT CLINIC

Michael Aling, Postindividualism: Fata Morgana and the Swindon Gout Clinic, Swindon, Wiltshire, 2009
above: Film stills of the gout clinic. In a documentary on the clinic, vignettes provide backdrops in which cinematic space has moved away from the perspectival (narcissistic, single point of view of Postmodernity) towards that of parallel projection. Axonometry is not simply a representational technique used to flatten depth on a page/screen, but a political ideology that erases the individualistic subject and allows for infinite entry points.

opposite top: A tophi operating theatre at the gout clinic. Tophi are common among Swindonians in the postindividualist age. Large crystalline deposits form on a variety of joints, from the shoulder to the helix of the ear. Such afflictions require surgical removal.

opposite bottom: Entrance hallway to the medical facility, under construction. Visitors often raise the similarities between the aesthetic of the clinic and the late 18th-century illustrations of 'The Gout' creature by James Gillray

The demographics of Swindon, a large provincial town in Wiltshire in southwest England, almost exactly match those of the entire UK population, being proportional in age, sex, ethnicity and income. The town can therefore be treated as a microcosm in which to test national social and spatial ideas. Historically, the death of the steam locomotive industry in the mid-20th century signalled the onset of the first 'iconoclasm' in Swindon (in terms of economic rather than religious erasure): the language of industrial architecture previously associated with the steam age became nothing more than nostalgic iconography, replaced with more relevant architectures as the postindustrial landscape ensued. With the current retail and financial sectors buckling under the weight of an economic meltdown, is the second iconoclasm of the railway town rearing its head? And in a failing economy, are the fiscal motifs of late capitalist architecture becoming redundant?

The Postindividualism: Fata Morgana and the Swindon Gout Clinic project focuses on a possible near future/visionary present of Swindon, in which the town undergoes a socioeconomic restructuring known as 'bipartite and tripartite individualism', more commonly referred to as 'postindividualism'.

The Postindividualism: Fata Morgana and the Swindon Gout Clinic project focuses on a possible near future/visionary present of Swindon, in which the town undergoes a socioeconomic restructuring known as 'bipartite and tripartite individualism', more commonly referred to as 'postindividualism'. In an act of desperation implemented by the local government, the population of Swindon has become conjoined individuals whereby two (bipartite) or three (tripartite) Swindonians share a name and profession. Working life is split into two models: a 'multiplicit' structure for office-based businesses in which conjoined individual(s) work(s) in parallel as the same virtual (computer ID) presence; and the 'omni-shift' model – a 24-hour (three stage/continual) shift for employees in industries such as construction and manufacturing. As the local authority creates more infrastructure projects, the economy expands as employment levels increase threefold and the population of 'individuals' seemingly reduces. Nevertheless, the retail sector, a major component of Swindon's economy, has been eradicated. Along with the rivalry of efficient Internet shopping, the population tends to use its spare time to undertake activities that assert individuality,

above: Film stills of the gout clinic. Towards the end of the documentary we realise that we are watching a film within the film, as one incarnation of the steadicam operator exits a cinema auditorium screening the documentary only to descend into the clinic that she had just been watching a documentary of, and appearing in. This reveal exposes the nature of enveloped production and consumption within the film industry and its impact on space outside that of the cinematic. Financially, the cinema will provide capital for the upkeep of the medical facility.

right: A panoramic ceilingscape structure built into the floor of the gout clinic. Due to the tricky vertical-tilt axis of the steadicam filming this scene for the documentary, a smooth camera pan is only achievable by tilting the lens below the camera operator (rather than above).

opposite: Although postindividualism claimed the death of consumer space, the subsequent retail mausoleums became infamous tourist attractions, creating a whole range of employment opportunities in both services and maintenance. In one such example, a polycarbonate ceilingscape is constructed with such low-quality materials that it is almost constantly being repaired.

Retail mausoleum. With the dust still settling from a recent re-enactment of a 'bargain hunt', those who mourn the death of retail wander the interior avenues of a consumerist iconoclasm.

A conjoined individual in Swindon, consisting of a middle-aged male, a single mother and a graduate. Acting as a single 'individual' in postindividualist Swindon on an omni-shift, they perform the role of a steadicam operator, employed to record the newly constructed gout clinic around the clock.

Film stills of retail mausoleum. Leaking pipes are encouraged in the former retail village, and the growth of stalactites is read as a conservation true to the original ideals of the building: cheap components and a short life span. Those who wander the mausoleum are said to experience Fata Morgana, a mirage in which space fractures into infinite breccia – desperate attempts from the subconscious to recall the glory days of shopping, sadly too undistinguished at the time to be truly remembered.

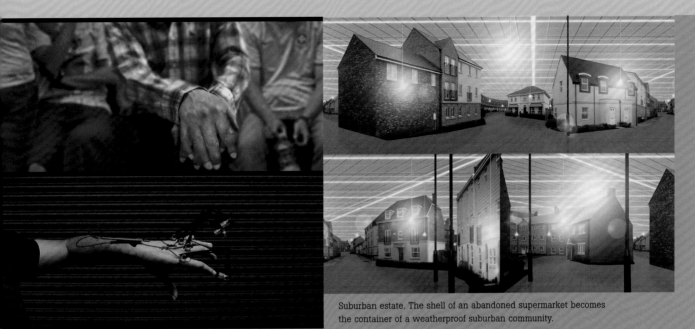

Suburban estate. The shell of an abandoned supermarket becomes the container of a weatherproof suburban community.

In a population rife with gout – the disease of consumption and excessive office hours swells the articulations of the masses – a seismographic glove can be worn to record the build-up of uric-acid crystals (tophi) in a patient's knuckle joints by scanning levels of friction as the fingers gyrate.

rather than erase it further through the consumption of indistinguishable products. With postindividualism came the death of consumer space in the physical, contingent sense.

However, the littered carcasses of retail have solved many sociospatial problems. One such example is how the growing population can find homes in a range of redeveloped retail spaces, from former supermarkets to overhauled high-street boudoirs. A number of these carcasses have become mausoleums for the few members of the public wishing to mourn retail's passing: mythic figures rumoured to attain levels of trance, witnessing Fata Morgana as a means to cope with their grief.

Of course postindividualism has had its fair share of criticism, given the assumption that individuality is their most treasured possession to all but a few. Somehow, though, the conjoining of individuals has had pleasing effects on the Swindonian postindividualists. The strategy itself took inspiration from Postmodern cinema and the reassumption that actors and their roles are not necessarily a coherent whole inside the narrative of a work. In many ways we are a population of performers: it has often been argued that we occupy a cinematic society, that we share collective screen memories and have developed a cinematic gaze, adopting the ocular lens of the film camera as a truthful way in which to perceive the world. If our experiences have taken their stimulus from cinema, can our architecture do the same? The popularity of Internet-based social networking strengthens our enjoyment in assessing one another as 'characters': vast numbers of people act out their chosen protagonist on the Internet, a fiction of themselves which they wish to exist in the public eye. Postindividualism functions in Swindon because every person is transformed into the status of a performer, acting out the (shared) major role from the screenplay of their life as they are living it.

What is peculiar is the surge in the recorded cases of gout in Swindon due to the superfluous freedoms and shared responsibilities of postindividualism. Causes of this particularly painful arthritic condition are said to vary from an increased intake of alcohol and a poorly regulated diet, to more elaborate tales of diets rich in fruit and root vegetables (the five-a-day schemes of the former supermarkets) ironically causing the disease to develop through increased fructose levels. The first newbuild in this postindividualist climate, a specialised gout medical facility, has thus been constructed to both combat the recent epidemic and fulfil the cinematic needs of a character-actor population – and is also the subject of a feature-length documentary, with the public as its protagonists. The articulations of the building romanticise the behaviour patterns of tophi, large uric-acid crystal formations on the joints of people suffering from advanced gout. Both beautiful and cruel, its architecture sympathises with patients as they occupy its body. And with lighting positioned to heighten the atmospherics of the *mise en scène*, and structures distanced to emphasise scale and field, the gout clinic proposes that the cinematic gaze is not simply a method by which to observe, but an instrument in itself for the construction of architecture. ⚙

OTAKU LIGHTING AND THE NOCTAMBULIST[1]

Street lighting extends the life of the city far beyond nightfall, perpetuating the day's activities while also making the metropolis a hub for leisure and entertainment. What if, however, it was necessary to curtail the use of electric lighting to conserve energy and to limit the impact of global warming? **John Culmer Bell**, founder of FXV, a studio concerned with researching the potential of new technologies and media in design, looks at how significant the lumination of the city is for urban culture.

JC Bell, Urban Otaku, 2009
Visualisation one of a series of designs for street furniture incorporating variable geometry and lighting which respond to electromagnetic fluctuations in the surrounding atmosphere. Developed from an earlier proposal by FXV.

In London, on Thursday 21 June 2007, in the evening between 21.00 and 22.00 the lights were turned out at Piccadilly Circus. It was the first time the lights had voluntarily been switched off since the Second World War. The gesture, part of a global initiative to raise awareness of global warming, was organised by a local radio station and supported by Friends of the Earth. Jenny Bates, from the environmental group, said:

> The majority of the capital's carbon dioxide emissions come from buildings, so switching off lights and appliances that aren't needed can play a significant role in tackling climate change. And it can save you money too.[2]

This seemingly uncontentious injunction to save energy is, I believe, worth a second glance, as it raises important issues for the future city. If we are to follow the line of thinking which informs current urban design practice, we will, in the near future, live in an efficiently illuminated, low-pollution continuum of well-directed moderate luminous intensity. Such a city will attempt to minimise its environmental impact, to achieve a relatively low carbon footprint and seek to promote and legislate for prudence in energy management: for a kind of stealth urbanism with a reduced Hertzian signature, a less obviously radiant metropolis.

But in moving towards an energy-efficient future, with its undoubted benefits, it is also prudent that prior to codifying or naturalising the rhetoric of 'environmental' lobbyists, we analyse our present urban conditions in order to formulate our aspirations for the future city, and in particular the future night-time city, which seems to be the target of current attention. To consider whether, or indeed how, efficiency should be measured. In order to act appropriately, it is worth considering the last great change in the lighting of the city, together with a glance at its programmatic and formal impacts and influences.

The introduction of electric lighting for urban areas in the late 19th and early 20th centuries must be seen to be hugely important. The then still novel *noctambulisme* – walking around at night for its own sake – was influential in the production of one urban intervention which exploited the new technology of electric light: the illuminated billboard. This transitional form, which arose out of the conflation of arc lighting and sign writing had, almost from its genesis, produced dissent through its brash intrusion into the night. Soon, the increasing efficiency and pliability of neon tubes extended the reach of the entertainment and advertising industries out from the material production of signage upon which light was

cast and into the production of a nightly evanescence: of light works that cohered to the evening activities of the growing number of city dwellers who, somewhat emancipated by technology, could afford to play for a while at night. By 1927 André Citroën could hire the Eiffel Tower and install his name in 125,000 lights.

Over the first decades of the 20th century, a bifurcation in the use of city lighting emerged: on the one side the historical trend for greater illumination to promote individual security, promulgated from the initial desire for street lighting to banish the shadows of the *mauvais garçons*[3] and their like, and on the other the new trend towards the exterior display of theatrical glamour, with advertising providing the lighting and urban scenography. Over the last hundred years or so, we have seen the emergence of particular zones of our cities which we associate with display. We can all name a few – London's Piccadilly Circus retains a certain celebrity, though its once ostentatious display has long been exceeded by others in New York and Tokyo, and indeed most major cities have their equivalents.

The critical importance of light as a monumental force in the city was clearly understood, even in the midst of the Second World War, incidentally the only preceding time when the Piccadilly lights were voluntarily extinguished. In 'Nine Points on Monumentality' (1943), Sert, Léger and Giedion wrote:

> During night hours, colour and forms can be projected on vast surfaces. Such displays could be projected upon buildings for purposes of publicity or propaganda. These buildings would have large plane surfaces planned for this purpose, surfaces which are non-existent today.[4]

This potential for light as monument, for civic illumination of a kind that exceeds that of mere utility, is annually rehearsed at festivals and celebrations, but its quotidian place is primarily understood in its use as an agency for civic pride: the floodlit facade or public artwork. While this is entirely reasonable, these illuminations point away from the inhabitants – light is borrowed through reflection, but the stars of the show are the ennobled objects, not the passers-by. It is in this regard that advertising illumination differs: it points at you, seeking to engage you directly, instantly, and to bypass critical faculties and seduce you at a preconscious level. In doing so it bathes you in light: it puts you on stage. As Walter Benjamin has noted: 'What, in the end, makes advertisements so superior to criticism? Not what the moving red neon sign says – but the fiery pool reflecting in the asphalt.'[5]

Illuminated advertising signage in Los Angeles.

The modern metropolis runs by virtue of infrastructures that have grown up in a period roughly contiguous with the development of urban illumination. Whatever diverse forces shape the future city, systems which carry information are and will continue to be critical. These grids run on photons: the functional space of the future city is primarily electromagnetic; electrical and electronic communications networks are essential in making contemporary cities possible, mediating the flows of capital, disseminating entertainment; and urban life is inconceivable without them. As Schivelbusch has noted, electrical power also tends to coincide with capital, which also seeks to move largely unseen:

> An analogy between electrical power and finance capital springs to mind. The concentration and centralisation of energy in high-capacity power stations corresponded to the concentration of economic power in big banks.[6]

Any overview of modern communications will show that, in terms of the electromagnetic spectrum, we have been moving through higher energy states and shorter wavelengths for the last century: from electrical waves, long-wave radio, up through FM and UHF to 3G and 4G networks, on to microwave relays and fibre channels, communications technologies are tending increasingly

From the ostentatious brick-like mobile phones of the 1980s, we now have communications and entertainment devices embedded in watches and glasses, projected as head-up displays in our cars and soon to be written directly on to the retina or emitted from a handy nano-projector enabled device.

towards the visible part of that spectrum. So our future is moderated by photons: historical trends point to this inevitability. For the most part these photons flash through fibre channels or move about us unseen: the connections of the city lie in barely visible, contiguous yet discrete webs. They almost always announce themselves privately. Communications technologies, our personal tools and toys, the tiny exfoliations of the communications grid, have scant visible impact at the level of the city; indeed, at every turn, the manifestations of informational infrastructures are at best a stealthy legion of innocuous boxes.

For instance, most urban mobile-phone masts are often more or less poorly camouflaged; there appears to

be a concerted denial of the very agencies that allow city life to exist; and mobiles, televisions, computers all tend towards material disappearance, being thinner, lighter, less substantial with each iteration, as if one day there will be only pure image. In a process which could be likened to the disappearance of the Cheshire cat, leaving only its grin, the physical apparatus of electronic communication seems set to dematerialise or to meld with cognate personal technologies. It loses its singular identity to become ubiquitous yet invisible. From the ostentatious brick-like mobile phones of the 1980s, we now have communications and entertainment devices embedded in watches and glasses, projected as head-up displays in our cars and soon to be written directly on to the retina or emitted from a handy nano-projector enabled device.

The democratisation of communications media is, of course, welcome. However, as the instruments which make the modern city possible obtrude less and less into its material landscape – as the telegraph pole gives way to the pico-cell and copper is replaced by glass – it seems reasonable to ask whether we should celebrate the primary mechanism of the city – whether a contemporary *genius loci* is either possible or desirable. The continuing popularity of iconic, hyperspecific urban phenomena, of the overlit, animated coruscating square, circus or crossing suggests that a 'spirit of place' in modern cities resides to a significant degree in the potential of light to confer a transient celebrity: places where we can clearly recognise that the apotheosis of the urban is its continual dissipation into electromagnetic radiation – and that it is doing it for us, the noctambulists, still drifting through the city after more than a hundred years.

Luminous facades have become the modern agencies for Benjamin's sublime answer to the critical: the Jumbotron, the supergiant screen, the retina-burning imprint of one's favourite product sliding around the corner. As the Situationists International told us: town planning is just an ideology in Marx's sense of the term; architecture is as real as Coca-Cola. When the visceral power of advertising coalesces at a sufficient intensity, then we go to see it, probably not so much to validate our latest beverage purchase as to witness the power of the city displayed for us. Environmentalists and planning authorities often see only one side of the energy equation: the costs of the ostensive programme and profligate expense to fuel non-essential advertisement. But we know that the maths is not that simple. Inasmuch as the impress of the electric sign on the city exceeds the critical in its affective immanence, we must understand this aspect of the urban as exceeding the normative logics of urban evaluation. We need to acknowledge that the magnetic attraction of people to big, bright lights is not just about buying stuff.

As we interrogate the datascape of the city and attempt to formulate apposite strategies for the future, we need better metrics – perhaps better tools with which we can capture programmatic nuance with as great a precision as geographical position. It is now mundane to know where you are; quite why you are there is generally a far more complex issue. This is not to slip into the metaphysical or ontological – it is a question of choice. Perhaps the contemporary fascination with locative technologies could offer some help in this regard – indeed some form

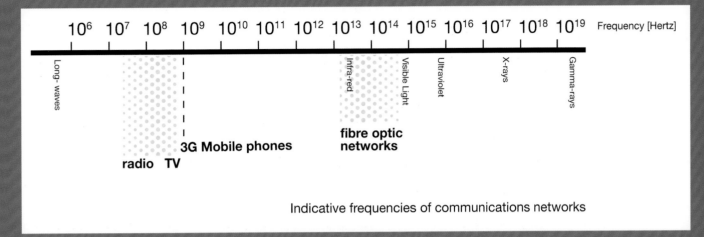

Indicative frequencies of communications networks

Diagram showing the operating zones of communications media in the context of the full electromagnetic spectrum.

of geotagged, XML-enabled swarm geography might one day emerge as a viable tool for urban analysis. Certainly polling organisations such as IPSOS MORI are using GPS units to track consumer travel and purchase habits in the run-up to the London Olympics.

Meanwhile, we have to be very careful of technologies such as Google's Streetview, where spotting signs of unsanctioned activity becomes a sport for geeks and censors with uncertain motives. We have seen a rash of more or less embarrassing activities revealed then scrubbed from Streetview, and disenchanted local residents driving the image-capture car out of town for fear of burglars and other unspecified scopically charged dangers. It is important to remind ourselves that these images are perennially out of date; despite attracting huge prurient interest, they merely render the city a sanitised snapshot.

Photons are hard to regulate and so are people. If we unthinkingly reach for the big switch without understanding the importance of the noctambulist, of the *flaneur*, of the free photon, our cities will be sadly impoverished. No more Times Square, no more Piccadilly Circus – a big city without its bright lights seems a lot less alluring. We all need playtime and a little light relief helps. As the cathedral once stood as the divine locus and imprimatur of the city, its aerial broadcasting to God, today's bright stages, the lights at the heart of every major city, must continue to burn. In the future we will still owe it to ourselves to radiate in the visible spectrum as intensely as possible. ⅅ

Notes

1. Around 1989, the term '*otaku*' entered colloquial use in Japan, applied in relation to a reclusive serial killer obsessed with pornographic anime and manga. As such it was intensely pejorative. Contemporary *otaku* people in Japan are defined more by their possessions than by their inherent character, particularly by their pathological attraction to certain media and technologies. In the West, *otaku* is seen as connoting extreme fandom, with fewer overtly negative connotations: it remains, though, a word associated with technology, obsession and alienation. However, *otaku* also, more traditionally, connotes house, home and family. It is an honorific term for one's organisation or may refer to someone of equal status.

2. BBC News report, 22 June 2007. See http://news.bbc.co.uk/1/hi/england/london/6225108.stm. However, this anodyne comment is more pernicious and indeed less accurate than it first appears. Since the birth of electric lighting, its use in public space has been a signal indicator of metropolitan vigour. The cost of lighting in the UK has declined and continues to do so: from around £6,600 per million lumen hours in 1800 – which was in turn 0.6 per cent of the cost in 1300. By 1900 the cost had fallen to £1,100 and by 2000 to just £1.70 per million lumen hours, approximately 1/4000th of the cost 200 years previously. This figure, though, is set to fall further: incandescent lamps have a luminous efficiency of around 17.5, meaning a 100-watt lamp produces 1,750 lumens, while a typical fluorescent fitting fares better with an index of 64. New LED technologies are soon to reach 350 – almost four times the luminous efficiency of the sun. The metrics of infrastructural auditing must be treated with extreme caution. A question beyond the scope of this piece, but which needs to be mentioned, is again driven by technology in the service of advertising. The near future will see the introduction of very low-energy digital paint technologies: any surfaces in the urban environment will become displays and will have a mutable appearance. This protean quality will no longer be consigned to the night: digital paint reflects light – like a book, it becomes easier to read by day.

3. *Mauvais garçons* (bad boys) roamed the Parisian streets prior to the introduction of public lighting. Used as a cipher for generalised nocturnal criminal threats.

4. José Lluís Sert, Sigfried Giedion and Fernand Léger, 'Nine Points on Monumentality', in S Giedion, *Architecture, You and Me: The Diary of a Development*, Harvard University Press (Cambridge, MA), 1958, pp 48–52.

5. Walter Benjamin, *Reflections*, Schocken Books (New York), 1986. Trans Edmund Jephcott.

6. Wolfgang Schivelbusch, *Disenchanted Night: The Industrialization of Light in the Nineteenth Century*, University of California Press (Los Angeles, CA), 1998.

The Groom's Gospel

The Groom's Gospel I

Bastian Glassner, a director at Lynn Fox, the makers of high-profile commercials and pop promotions, summons up a simultaneously sumptuous and visceral vision – The Groom's Gospel. For this new project, produced for this publication in January 2009, guts and innards make the improbable transformation into delicate baroque forms.

The Groom's Gospel II

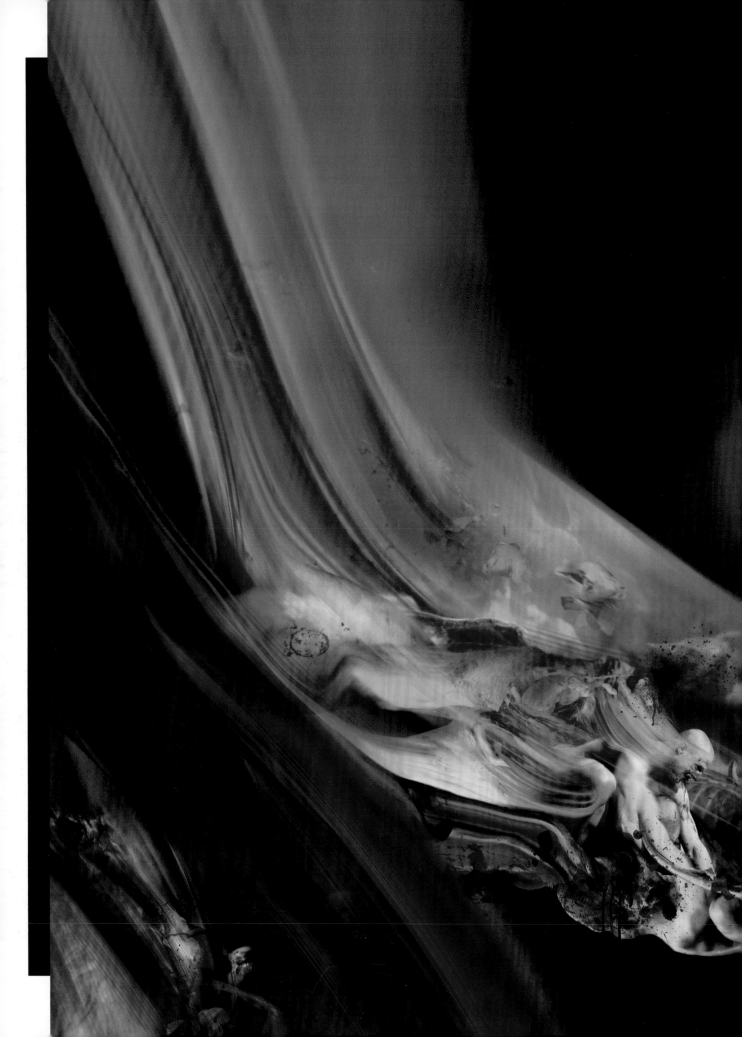

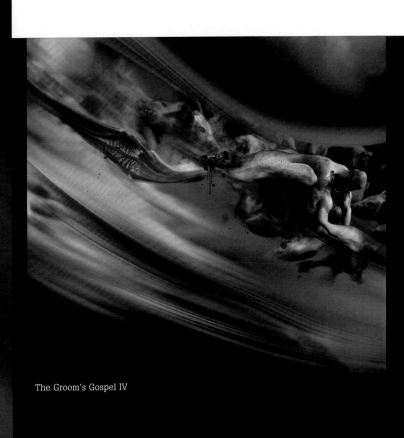

The Groom's Gospel IV

When you make the two into one, and when you make the inner like the outer and the outer like the inner, and the upper like the lower, and when you make male and female into a single one, so that the male will not be male nor the female be female, when you make eyes in place of an eye, a hand in place of a hand, a foot in place of a foot, an image in place of an image, then you will enter [the kingdom].

Stephen Patterson and Marvin Meyer, 'The "Scholars' Translation" of the Gospel of Thomas', from *The Complete Gospels: Annotated Scholars Version*, 1994[1]

Here is to you then, saliva of dreams, fever of rotten veins, puss of the universe. I spit on you my feeble friend. Don't come close. I'm full of spots and ulcers. Rivers of tears are flushing those shit-covered drainpipes that are my guts. The stench of this vile brew is making me faint. Shall beasts rain on you, you young prince. You!

Lurid angels swirling above as I thirst for the burning thighs of thee queen. My grave closing in, the knights are galloping, poised to get me … *Monsters*!

Quick, you shout, a word about distance: there the virtuoso dance of the real disappears if faced by distance. It dissolves in favour of a schematic and rather predictable generalisation of the unfamiliar. Heavenly littered with gore your pitiful afterbirth, yet so nice and lively and after all in full-blown colour. But let us lay off that filthy soup for that your skin should shine like the jack-light of old. Oh how we love it dearly when E-ffects are mere reflections of profound truths carved in ancient headstones elsewhere. Or is it A-ffects in this instance? After all, lust strives for distance and blossoms best when delayed. Quick is the attempt to defer it. Coitus interruptus! Nothing but the monstrous

The Groom's Gospel III

The Groom's Gospel VI

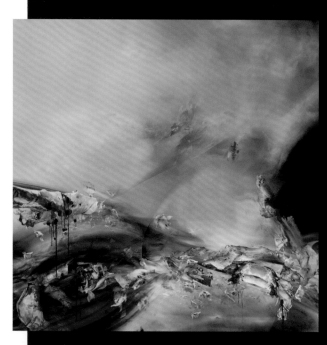

The Groom's Gospel XI

byproduct of the butchers at work. Ball lightning shall be thrashing through your entrails. I hope your rod falls off. Oh saviour, you cleanly decapitated pig, offer me your dripping placenta at least!

Herein then lies the task: the heavily pregnant mythical imaginary can't be slashed nor gutted or disembowelled by the representation of a deliberately structured fact. No relief to be found by indulging in the system of real relations that determine this existence, but by the make-believe's correlation of such existence in relation to its rather real condition. Laughter is the anatomy of pain.

What do you mean, excess? What remains is nothing but a loose assembly of close-ups that cover every insignificant limb with an obscene aura of disgusting details. A tumour-infected rectum! Let toxic haemorrhoids bleed like deadly projectiles. Heavenly redemption on all shores thus. Finally an unrestricted dedication to the banal. Now that is quite something!

A space of loss? Questionable!

Rather a step sideways: there just isn't anything to be found other than rot, and after all one better stays at home and enjoys the comfort of the warm oven. Hellfire! Dirge or laughter? Enough farts from the lardy pikes. Nothing is better than a clear syntax. Here, though, the pleasant ointment of rare *Essences* still thrives. What we need is not a higher birthrate, but more excess of sperm. And yes, one *Figure* or another of something read, overheard or lived cannot be denied amid all this dissolute flesh. *Erinyes* stay revengeful, regardless how well imbedded in righteous *Topos*. Gimme *Monsters*, gimme *Monsters*!

Now over to the loss of myths, hurry, hurry: the burning flesh is too scared to follow function and two systems of magical procreation keep irritating one another over and over without ever being able to merge entirely. Sort of an infinite Euclidean dilemma, a rancid moon, Ophelia incapable of her own distress.

In that case much rather like pornographically stated: Let us be lovers! If in wild thought the imaginary is the prize which the symbolic order has to pay for it to survive the jungle, then the symbolic has to vanish entirely so a pure mysticism can re-territorialise.

Well conceived reason? Probably just an invitation. You may laugh. As obscure as it may sound: only when the dead body is dissected in its entirety can it be resurrected and its testicles be recoded. Hail the chimes of myths. Out there somewhere are leprosy-shredded extremities, forever drifting helpless through the boiling fever pits of the epicurean soup.

Along floats a faint shadow. Luminously quiet and backwards plays his castrated voice: Oh yes I spit on thee! Drench your soul in my pest-infested saliva.

I am the Groom. ⚭

Note
1. Stephen Patterson and Marvin Meyer, 'The "Scholars' Translation" of the Gospel of Thomas', from *The Complete Gospels: Annotated Scholars Version*, Polebridge Press, 1994.

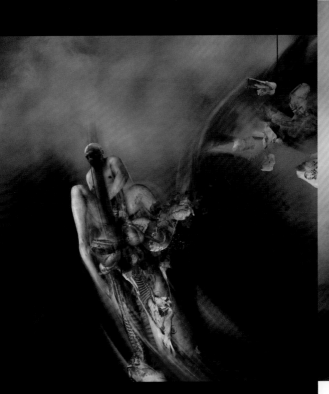

The Groom's Gospel VII

The Groom's Gospel X

The Groom's Gospel XII

The Groom's Gospel XIII

Hong Kong

concrete landscape by land value

the high poplation to land area ratio in hong kong makes land very precious. in particular the peak and the harbour-front. the invaluable victoria harbour view caused uncontrolled reclamation and uncontrolled building heights to generate the most economical value. as a result, victoria harbour has became victoria lane, a street that walled by two rows of ultra-tall residential highrises. the building heights decrease away from the ex-harbour, and increase again towards the peak and other water fronts.

The new landscape of Hong Kong where building heights are primarily determined by economic values rather than effective building control regulations.

Labyrinths

In this set of film stills, **Soki So** recasts the tangled density of Hong Kong's high-rises as Piranesi's 'Carceri'. It is a hyper-realism that magnifies and intensifies the urban experience, highlighting the precariousness of current environmental and social conditions.

Bird's-eye view revealing how Victoria Lane was formed by the construction of taller towers closer to Victoria Harbour.

Soki So, Hong Kong Labyrinths, Hong Kong, China, 2048
left: Chronogram. Concept drawing depicting conditions at different levels, vertically down Victoria Lane. The diagram maps temporal flow, as well as events and spatial order for the construction of the film.

opposite: Uniformly distributed ceiling lights and billboards create the illusion of exterior daylighting.

Crawford

the illusion of daylighting

The day and night inhabitation patterns inherited from Hong Kong's culture of timlessness – a survival practice to cope with the unbearable heat during the day. Interior adaptations include the excessive use of air-conditioning and insulation on redundant window openings.

When the ever-shrinking Victoria Harbour finally became the Victoria Lane and the tallest buildings were raised on the most valuable, and what was once the lowest, surface of the city the geographic profile of Hong Kong had changed for ever and a new ecology was formed.

Hot air accumulated between the buildings due to their proximity to one another. Heat during the day, when the sun was at its most powerful, became unbearable.

Buildings designed with thick concrete walls attempted to block out the heat from the outside, and functionless window openings inherited from long-outdated building ordinances were covered with insulation.

Staying in the air-conditioned interior helped, but was not enough. People started to rest during the day when temperatures were too high for them, and woke up at night as they had been accustomed to in the past, when they worked, played mahjong or wandered around the games centres from evening to early morning.

Exterior became a concept rather than an actual site for inhabitation, but maybe it did not matter any more; they did not need to go out, as there was always an enclosed route to go anywhere.

In future Hong Kong, things changed, but versatility ruled and it was as if people had lived like this for years.

the abandonned exterior and walled city

Abandoning the exterior. Victoria Lane being used as a dumping ground
in relation to the uncontrolled reclamation in Victoria Harbour.

timeless social systems and indirect communications

The excessive use of electronic communications devices that disregard physical proximity
and time shift the temporal inhabitation pattern to create a new social context.

residue and by-product of unquestioned practice

as construction period in urban regeneration with demolishing old buildings takes time and money, new building is built directly on top of the existings to jump through the process for efficiency at both time and economical aspects. windows in future hong kong are the residue of unquestioned building regulation in the past, which now being used as spaces to place air handling units. All of these has become the new architectural language in future hong kong.

Conditions at the abandoned level where old buildings are buried under out-of-scale new constructions; the consequence of unorganised urban regeneration practices.

Hong Kong, being a city with one of the highest population densities in the world, employs high-rise buildings, reclamation of the harbour and multilayered circulations as generic urban regeneration strategies to cope with the rapidly growing population within the limited urban space. However, after years of misuse these practices have turned into unquestioned and uncontrolled routines. The mundane and uncritical n processes fail to maintain any form of organised urban planning, and no attempt is being made to balance economic and environmental values, or development and conservation.

The emergence of the hundred-storey towers at the Hong Kong harbour front has been of great economic value; however, it has also caused serious environmental issues, particularly in terms of inner-city air quality. The involvement of local communities in urban design is often overlooked, avoided or even bypassed by developers and statutory bodies in order to speed up building projects. Many well-developed neighbourhoods have been forced to break down under compulsory reallocation schemes, which have not only caused social deconstruction at both the macro and micro scales, but have also led to the disappearance of local history and cultures. If development continues along these lines, a new method of occupying the city will be needed to cope with the climatic and cultural changes caused by the system. Hong Kong Labyrinths is a film project that speculates on an extreme environment created out of the current situation in Hong Kong. It is a proposal for survival that explores a new model of time-shifted inhabitation, adapted to the projected climatic, cultural and social environments that are the consequences of the city's current uncritical architectural systems and practices. By using film as the medium, the tangibility and familiarity of a shifted temporal occupation that responds to the possible new relationship between interior and exterior is tested dynamically against the knowledge and sensibility of the audience.

In addition, the film deliberately investigates the visual and experiential connection between proposed speculation and the infamous Kowloon Walled City, which existed as an iconic symbol of density and unorganised planning in Hong Kong between the 1940s and 1990s. It asks whether the past conditions have been reformed in contemporary systems, and questions whether the current architectural practices and systems are generative, regenerative or degenerative. Δ

Distructuring Utopias

Rubedo, The Hive, London, 2009
The ubiquitous network culture is the Hive Mind
embodied. While swarm systems, like particle
fields, are adaptable and resilient emergent
organisations, they are also non-optimal,
unpredictable, uncontrollable and do not allow
for individuality, transgression or excess.

In order to meet the challenges of fast-paced urban transformations, **Laurent-Paul Robert and Dr Vesna Petresin Robert** of Rubedo call for a rethinking of the perennial Utopian model of urban design. They espouse a design strategy that is both able 'to reflect the dynamics of urban growth and decay', while meeting the needs of a 'post-capitalist economy' — a condition in which change is the only constant.

The Demise of Utopias?

Anticipation of near futures heightens at times of economic and social collapse and the dissolution of dominant value systems. A place of perfection, indefinitely removed from reality and fuelled by optimism and a need for alternative futures, Utopia[1] brings a consensual hallucination of an ambiguous value: its implicit perfection signals a futile expectation of a better future. Utopian towns may never have been truly global, have never radically challenged social and moral conventions or allowed anonymous existence. However, there is no doubt that speculations and attempted constructions of an ideal city – be it Atlantis, Filarete's Sforzinda, the Garden Cities of the Industrial Revolution, CIAM's Functional City, the Chinese People's Communes or Marshall McLuhan's Global Village – have nevertheless had an impact on urban landscapes and lifestyles.

While the trend forecast remains predominantly city-oriented,[2] postindustrial cities tend to develop by responding to the unpredictable dynamics of the market and society – not necessarily in the way dreamt up by their planners. Form is a result of feedback information: complex patterns emerge from the capacity for self-organising and adaptive behaviours. Architects are no longer the only ones determining functional and symbolic aspects of space. This role is increasingly being taken over by engineers, software developers and inhabitants themselves.

But fast-paced urban transformations also call for a fresh perspective: complex urban structures require a design strategy to reflect the dynamics of urban growth and decay and to anticipate a postcapitalist economy. Rather than keeping inevitable changes at bay by means of planning, urban as well as social networks are embracing change as a fundamental condition, and perhaps the only constant.

Are utopian models still relevant or should they be dismissed as mere ideological constructs?

Cities have been trapped in a cycle of demolition and reconstruction for centuries, but the short-term political effects of urban rebranding often leave behind a number of conservationist or social issues, as well as a trail of structures past their sell-by date – what Rem Koolhaas calls 'JunkSpace'.[3]

Can a relevant utopian model still emerge in the current condition? Existing reality can only be altered by introducing models that make the old ones obsolete, rather than eradicating them by decree. As novelty is thought to arise from an unfamiliar organisation of existing material, can we consider any emerging urban models to be truly new?

While utopias can offer a polygon for creative speculation in times of crisis, their power as well as failure lies in their play with our fears and desires. History shows that uncritically embraced utopias result in ever greater disasters,[4] while the rigorous urban planning interventions they inspire reflect the lowest level of democracy.

Instruments of Power and Control

Technology as a Vehicle of Social and Political Power
Architecture, through the interaction of its symbolic and physical spatial components, is inseparable from manifestation of power. The economic, technological, political or religious systems that embody power exercise control through projections of an unattainably perfect future. Such instruments of control and technological dominance are usually accompanied by fear and submission, but also revolt and transgression; from the fortresses of medieval Europe to 21st-century urban bunkers, their architecture seems to be a manifestation of paranoia.

Ideologies are by definition effective in constructing spaces of false identification. Technology, like any ideology, thrives on dreams of mobility, power and omnipresence; to some extent, this may be an enactment of the denial of death, a chance to reboot, to replay an event and to try a different resolution.

Though Buckminster Fuller[5] may have advocated the power of technology to promote social change, it has become, through the prism of the rituals of the industrial age, a quasi-religious subject.[6]

Belief in technology is a quick escape from the trauma of the ultimate server crash – our mortality. And yet it merely offers an instant, substitute liberation from social and existential constraints.

In Lacanian terms,[7] the reality of utopia is a phantasmic 'passionate attachment', a traumatic scene that never actually took place. Real is the traumatic essence of the Same; we try to escape from it through virtual, fantastic and symbolic universes. Resisting symbolisation and dialectical mediation could therefore bring a release from the myth of the power of technology.

The Current Condition – A Hotbed for Utopias

The present lack of structure between organic and synthetic life, local communities and the global flow of data, workforce and capital invites an excess of utopian, dystopian and heterotopian visions. The situation is not dissimilar to periods of decline of Modernist utopias promising individuals development and fulfilment within society that gave us a Futurist discourse of a non-organic future[8] as well as the phenomenon of virtual environments.

Urban Transformations

Late capitalism has fabricated a borderless, accelerated space based on the flow, manipulation and transformation of capital. As a consequence of new production modes, digital culture, the miniaturisation of technology and the impact of online communities on urban lifestyles, urban landscapes have been dramatically transformed.

Space, no longer shaped merely by boundaries but increasingly by network connectivity, requires us to redefine the foundations of architectural theory and practice. As transformation and growth has resulted in the spatial dispersal of economic activities, a new matrix of the information society with centralised power has emerged. However, new forms of marginality and polarisation have also been taking shape. Urban territories are being reorganised and renegotiated, while spatial metadata and the related technologies are gaining importance.

Exploring an Alternative, Deep Space

The development of technologies away from the surface of the earth has enabled the evolution of global communications that have brought social changes and stimulated the exploration of alternative environments. As the near future brings extreme existential and social conditions, extending urban activities into such alternative environments could become an important strategy.[9]

Exploring and colonising deep space as well as alternative habitats on earth remains the final frontier. Although seemingly introducing a different spatial discourse, cyberspace was the result of an intense reduction: a process of abstracting perceptions of the world that had begun with the Cartesian grid. With its lack of spatial and temporal reference points, weight and boundaries, cyberspace has prepared the ground for considering deep space as an alternative habitat.[10]

An exploration of new territories and forms of autarchic collective dwelling may engage us with the biggest issues of the present rather than fictitious, metaphysical space – it may even initiate a new humanism.

The Pervasive Influence of Digital Culture

While the Enlightenment may have viewed universalism as an instrument of uninhibited growth and progress, the globalisation via technological, economic and information exchange promoted dislocation, fragmentation and uniform, homogenised thought. Social structure, as well as the boundaries of our identities and our sense of self, have become fluid.

The desire for movement is essentially a search for freedom, fuelled by new energy sources, new means of transportation and new technologies. It can trigger social mobility and 'distructuring'[11] along with new forms of collective dwelling. While capital enabled a mobilisation of values, objects and ideologies, economy is now driven by information exchange.

Communications infrastructures have become a lever of contemporary global economic systems, supported by technologies that neutralise distance and the notion of place. In the search for a sense of place, the future – just like a computer screen – is a territory that lies in front of us. Progress is synonymous with moving forward; thus, the dominance of our sense of vision is amplified while our objectivity is diminished.

The information society is rooted in voyeurism and escapism. The effect of constant media saturation is similar to perceiving a multitude of stimuli simultaneously. The omnipresent Orwellian viewer desires technological supremacy and a capacity for surveillance that brings power and God-like control.

The information society is rooted in voyeurism and escapism. The effect of constant media saturation is similar to perceiving a multitude of stimuli simultaneously. The omnipresent Orwellian viewer desires technological supremacy and a capacity for surveillance that brings power and God-like control. But while this is a detached, non-interventionist position where the only 'real' experience is the one that has been mediated, in the quantum universe, on the other hand, it is the observer who influences the observed and vice versa. Such experience is personal and subjective, and moves away from a logic of discursive intellect, or the causality of Euclidean space.

The predominantly time-based media of the information society show the observer rather than the observed, thus enhancing the subjectivity of experience. 'Reality' is an illusion, a fabrication.[12] Information technology influences our perceptions and constructs forms of control. By creating a new interface between the self, the other and the world beyond, it also constructs our reality. On the other hand, the saturation of the mass media is causing increased distrust, indicating a general crisis of representation. The flood of computer-generated images and simulations of this brave new world has triggered a fear of losing real territory.

Rubedo, Heterotopia, London, 2009
The demise of the non-anthropomorphic environment
and the information structure prepared the ground for a
condition 'from the middle out', where phenomena are
not separate from their representations. If capital is no
longer the driving force of urban organisations, what
alternative forms will collective dwelling take?

Rubedo, Qaniyatu Elima I, London, 2009
The notion of intimacy is a public commodity. The utmost private space – the inner body – is in the public domain, accessible and marketable via communications technologies.

A Hive Mind

Tribal Organisations

A hybrid society that is simultaneously an individual and a collective place has its origins in the communities and social structures that developed online.[13] In a return to clans and tribal lifestyles, the association of individuals is no longer based on nationality, religion or social class, but on common interests and goals.

While representative and nation-state-based democracies are decaying and the globalised economy is withdrawing, elements of hybrid urban space are increasingly configured by their users rather than their designers. Technology does not necessarily develop as its designer envisaged, and architects might no longer be the only ones determining the functional and symbolic aspects of spatial organisations.[14]

Eroding the Boundaries Between Nature and Culture

In an attempt to produce a critique of the anaemic aesthetics of media space, the search for the organic is reflected in fascination with artificial intelligence, neuron networks, bio- and nanotechnology, and particle physics. Preoccupation with scale is characterised by its absence, or by investigation of its extremes. Architecture moves towards customised models, embedded with bio- and nanotechnologies rather than their mechanical counterparts, thus slowly erasing the boundaries between the organic and the man-made.[15]

The global tech culture aims at eradicating differentiation and establishing a world where reference to the natural is obsolete.

The global tech culture aims at eradicating differentiation and establishing a world where reference to the natural is obsolete.[16] This ideology of technological progress promises to liberate our suffering bodies from desire and death. Its origins can be detected in Greek mechanistic cosmology: Heron's automata and architecture of war machines prepared the ground for the philosophy of Descartes, and the belief that engineering excellence can manifest a better future.

The myth of an engineered utopia has been spread by the Bible's call to conquer nature and the apocalyptic vision of a New Jerusalem, as well as the Protestant work ethic. Workaholism along with techno-utopianism and perfectionism all share faith in a world of limitless

potential for improvement. Similarly, Modernity is characterised, to a certain extent, by the conceptual barrier erected between nature and culture. According to this worldview, technology is a passive extension of the human, strengthening our creative capacities at the expense of our natural abilities.

The *Myth of the Machine*[17] insists on the authority of technical and scientific elites; it reinforces the value of efficiency, material progress, control and technological development, of economic and territorial expansion. But these ideals may conceal ambitions that lead to ecological catastrophe.

Emerging Models of Spatial Organisation

Models of planning for cities of global capital flow have been exhausted. But such a crisis may be recognised as a positive moment before reorganisation and restructuring, with new patterns and networks emerging from chaotic states. While ambiguity and chaos signal anticipation of change in our perceptive apparatus, and therefore danger and possible collapse, conservation on the other hand preserves a particular state by preventing evolution. To integrate change within our activities rather than obstruct it would mean integrating conflict as a constructive force; allowing a move away from a state of stasis redefines chaos as an evolutionary, creative process.

An open-ended, bottom-up approach where error is a valuable though unexpected alternative is inclusive. In social, geopolitical and economic terms, it initiates a structure with no centre and no margin. Including error as a local condition may also represent a valuable step in the evolution of an aesthetic in an attempt to steer away from the notion of algorithmic perfection.

Building self-sufficient units and reconsidering the typology of collective dwelling in analogy with complex adaptive systems[18] could help generate new, more sustainable forms of living. The scale of structures and organisations is critical in preventing architecture from becoming merely biomimetic.[19] Learning from Le Corbusier's *Le Modulor*, architecture may ultimately avoid becoming enslaved by its algorithms. While scripting formal as well as performative aspects of structural elements is normative, the local, the individual and the particular that influence the global through juxtaposition should be taken into consideration.

An extended notion of architecture as an increasingly collaborative endeavour requires innovation enabled by associative, bottom-up approaches. An open-ended design process in adaptive structural systems allows the consideration of all available options from the start while reducing risks. Space thus becomes shaped by information and architecture becomes synonymous with trans-scalar design.

New Uses of Space and Time Informed by Technology

The information society, organised around abstract values (numeric, audio and visual data), reintegrates time with space. Sets of time-based parameters such as sound, movement or behaviour have become building materials. Large data sets and real-time data can be dynamically visualised using animation and interactivity, and a certain type of representation can be mapped into another: image into sound,

sound into space. New representations therefore initiate not only new paradigms, but also transform the design process and modes of production.

However, as differences between local/distant, inside/outside, time/space, body/mind, real/imaginary cannot be clearly defined, many physical attributes in representation have, according to Manovich,[20] been replaced by meta-attributes. Representation requires consideration of its antithesis. Consolidating the being-in, being-there, immediate real-time visualisation as well as just-in-time production without prototype allows a degree of immersion that makes representation redundant and also reinforces the concept of a continuous present.

Design After Representation

Just-in-time customisation is flexible and adaptive, based on demand rather than the marketing of finalised products or buildings. Rapid prototyping might be replaced by immediate customised crafting as a direct response to individual needs or community needs.[21] Unlike in a consumption society, users are becoming creative by definition.

Reimagining forms of representation for processes and phenomena that are intangibly small or infinitely large might ensure designing in a 4-D space without dimensional reductions; simulacrum would thus become actualisation. This world of extreme scalarity might also initiate its own processes of abstraction and symbolic representation, generating new cultural paradigms.

An information-based economy is emerging in which the exchange of data takes place without an intermediate. If capital and the state-based economy disappear, cities may cease to be a viable form of dwelling, requiring new spatial, geopolitical, cultural and economic organisations.

An information-based economy is emerging in which the exchange of data takes place without an intermediate. If capital and the state-based economy disappear, cities may cease to be a viable form of dwelling, requiring new spatial, geopolitical, cultural and economic organisations.[22] However, appreciating immaterial as a material condition and allowing the acceptance of error, failure and demise could prevent a descent into technocratic totalitarianism and sustainably link architectural tradition to its future. ⌂

Notes
1. Thomas Moore, *Utopia*, Penguin Books (London), 1969.
2. Deyan Sudjic, 'Cities on the Edge of Chaos', *Observer*, 9 March 2008. Sudjic argues that today there are more cities on the planet that are larger than they have ever been in history. In the 19th century, an estimated 10 per cent of the population lived in cities, but by 2001 the proportion had increased to 50 per cent. 70 per cent of today's urban population can be found in emergent economies, due to the transformation of traditional forms of dwelling and the related activities (such as migration).
3. Rem Koolhaas, 'Junkspace', in *Content*, Taschen (New York), 2004.
4. Duanfang Lu, 'Third world modernism: utopia, modernity, and the people's commune in China', *Journal of Architectural Education*, Vol 60/3, 2007, p 41. Duanfang Lu comments: 'The Chinese People's Commune movement can be looked at as a concrete manifestation of the high modernist vision. Built on fantasies of industrial and social modernity, commune modernism was directed by a faith in the possibility of overcoming the past to create a brand new world. Like many high modernist experiments in other parts of the world, however, the mass utopia only left a history of disasters in its wake.'
5. Richard Buckminster Fuller, *Utopia or Oblivion: The Prospects for Humanity*, Allen Lane (London), 1970.
6. David F Noble, *The Religion of Technology*, Alfred A Knopf (New York), 1997.
7. Slavoj Zizek, 'The Cyberspace Real', see http://www.egs.edu/faculty/zizek/zizek-the-cyberspace-real.html. See also: Slavoj Zizek, *On Belief*, Routledge (London), 2001.
8. Filippo Tommaso Marinetti, 'The Founding and Manifesto of Futurism', *Le Figaro* (Paris), 20 February 1909. See also: Antonio Sant'Elia, 'Manifesto of Futurist Architecture', 1914, as published in Umbro Apollonio (ed), *The Documents of Twentieth Century Art: Futurist Manifestos*, Viking Press (New York), 1973.
9. Stephen Baxter, *Deep Future*, Victor Gollancz (London), 2002.
10. Michael Benson, 'A Look Back at Day Zero', *Leonardo Electronic Almanach*, Vol 8, No 2, February 2000. See http://mitpress.mit.edu/e-journals/LEA/AUTHORS/ZG/zero-G.html.
11. 'Distructure', as defined by Andree C Ehresmann and J-P Vanbremeersch, *Memory Evolutive Systems: Hierarchy, Emergence, Cognition*, Elsevier (Amsterdam and Oxford), 2007, and by Mark Cousins, 'Distructure' lecture series, Architectural Association, London, 27 February to 20 March 2009.
12. Ada Louise Huxtable, *The Unreal America: Architecture and Illusion*, New Press (New York), 1999. In *The Unreal America*, Huxtable expresses fears over a state of illusion, often perpetuated by multinational chain stores, that people started to favour over reality to the point where the replica is accepted as genuine and the simulacrum replaces the source.
13. Florian Roetzer, 'Our Space or Virtual Space? Utopias of the Digital Age', in J Beckmann, *The Virtual Dimension: Architecture, Representation, and Crash Culture*, Princeton Architectural Press (New York), 1998.
14. William J Mitchell, *Me ++: The Cyborg Self and the Networked City*, MIT Press (Cambridge, MA), 2003.
15. Ray Kurzweil, *Age of Spiritual Machines: How Will We Live, Work, Think in the New Age of Intelligent Machines*, Texere (New York and London), 2001.
16. Erik Davis, *TechGnosis: myth, magic + mysticism in the age of information*, Serpent's Tail (London), 1999.
17. Lewis Mumford, *Myth of the Machine: Technics and Human Development*, Harcourt (New York), 1971.
18. Stephen Johnson, *Emergence: The Connected Lives of Ants, Brains, Cities, and Software*, Scribner Book Company (New York), 2002.
19. Kevin Kelly, *Out of Control: The New Biology of Machines, Social Systems and the Economic World*, Perseus Books (New York), 1995.
20. Lev Manovich, *The Poetics of the Augmented Space: Learning from Prada*, 2002, updated 2005. See http:// http://www.manovich.net /TEXTS_07.HTM.
21. Rubedo with Philip Delamore (LCF Digital Fashion Studio, University of Arts London), *Developing 3D parametric modelling technology to create innovative surface pattern for the fashion and textiles sector*, Creative Industries Feasibility Study, Technology Strategy Board – Department of Innovation, 2009.
22. Antonio Negri, *Time for a Revolution*, Continuum International Publishing Group – Academi (London), 2003.

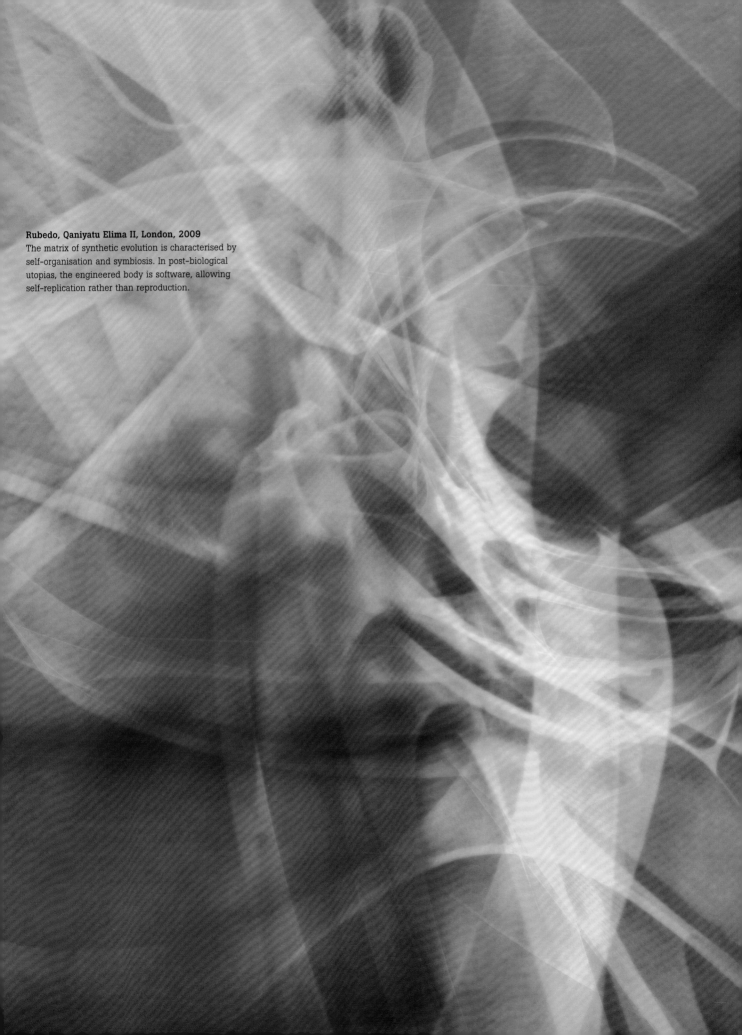

Rubedo, Qaniyatu Elima II, London, 2009
The matrix of synthetic evolution is characterised by
self-organisation and symbiosis. In post-biological
utopias, the engineered body is software, allowing
self-replication rather than reproduction.

THE CARBON CASINO

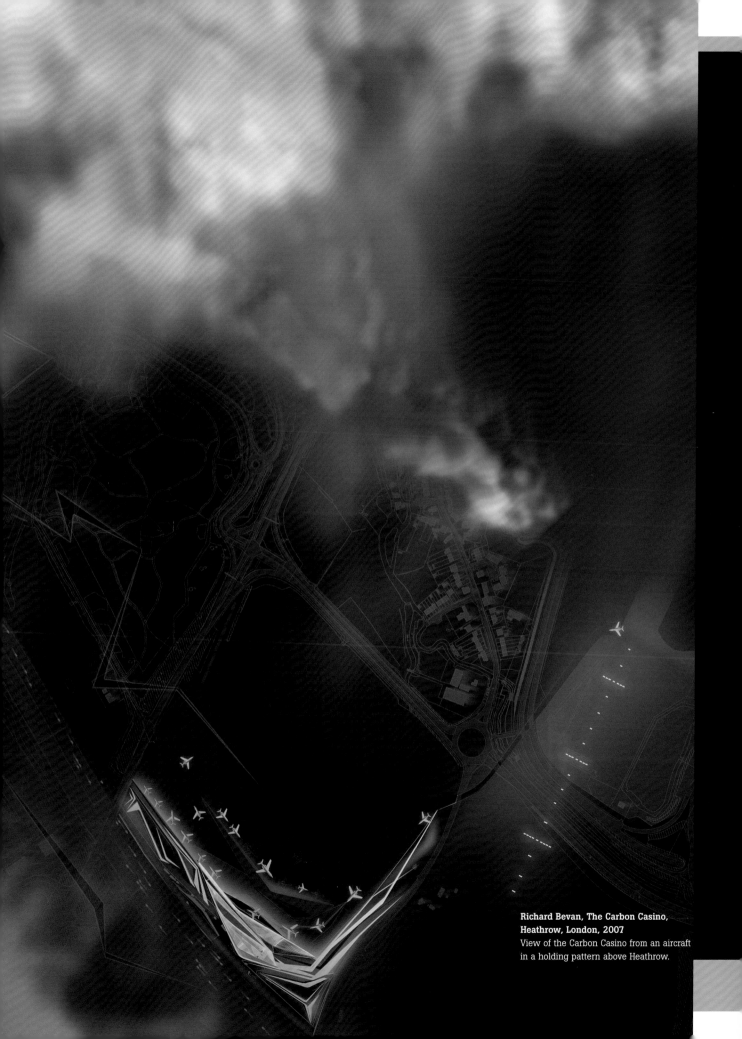

**Richard Bevan, The Carbon Casino,
Heathrow, London, 2007**
View of the Carbon Casino from an aircraft
in a holding pattern above Heathrow.

Richard Bevan re-imagines Heathrow Airport in 2030. In an age where Personal Carbon Allowances (PCAs) have become the dominant currency, the facilities at Heathrow are turned over to a carbon casino that affords airside and landside customers the opportunities to participate in gambling with the relevant tax breaks applied.

By the year 2030, carbon emissions will be fundamental to the function of society. Estimates for required UK carbon emissions reductions vary from around 70 per cent towards nearly 90 per cent of present levels by 2030 as part of a global drive to balance carbon emissions against the biosphere's capacity to absorb carbon. The introduction of Personal Carbon Allowances (PCAs)[1] will spread the emissions responsibility more evenly between individuals as well as business and government. In doing so, localised economies will prosper as transactions become place specific.

In the field of transport, Heathrow Airport Organisation Ltd (HAO Ltd) will continue to be subjected to increasingly intense emissions standards protocols, requiring balance through carbon offsetting. European air quality limits to be imposed in 2010 will increase significantly by 2020 and are set to rise again in 2030. This cost is unserviceable if HAO Ltd is to remain an effective, profitable and competitive transport corporation.

As a panacea to predicted near-future financial problems, it is proposed that latent opportunity exists in a unique facility that would utilise and further interface the transient populations of both Heathrow and the M25.

Transaction and trading opportunity could be accommodated between a wide range of existing Heathrow and adjacent M25 businesses and consumers. The proposal seeks to interface these consumers within a luxurious entertainment-based casino environment to facilitate PCA trading. Customers wishing to

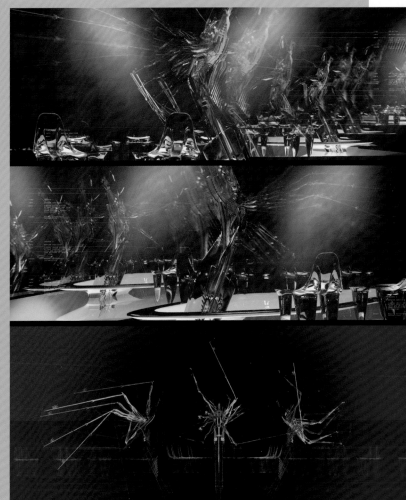

purchase extra PCA credit to allow for additional international travel can trade with customers wishing to sell excess/accumulated annual PCA credit. These transactions will all be accommodated within a casino environment that encourages carbon-based gambling. In doing so, the facility would hybridise both casino and carbon trading mechanisms: a carbon trading casino.

Consumer research suggests locating this facility along the eastern edge of the M25 between the main Heathrow turnoff and Junction 15. Airside- and landside-based consumers could be accommodated within a pseudo trading/casino environment that straddles both boundaries, allowing for legal and tax advantages associated with airside retail trading.

Dealer robot used on the gaming podiums within the Carbon Casino.

Example Transaction Parties

Airside purchasers of PCA credit
1 High net worth individuals landing at Heathrow in private aircraft.
2 Frequent international travellers.

Landside sellers of PCA credit
1 Daily M25 users with minimal long-distance travel.
2 London-based residents with minimal long-distance travel.

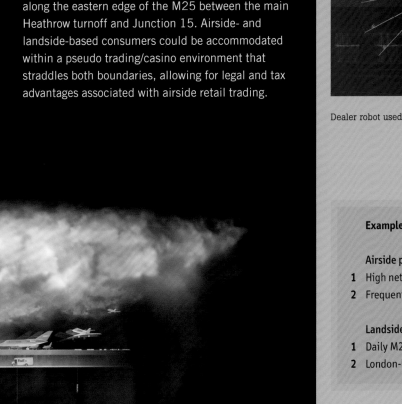

Long section view of the Carbon Casino with airside access on the right and landside access on the left.

Security screens used within
the security facility in the belly
of the Carbon Casino.

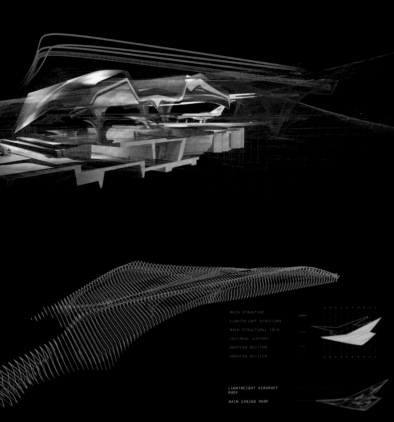

All Carbon Casino customers will be given the opportunity to trade at preferable capping rates relative to existent online/international trading houses. However, far superior values will be on offer to consumers who select transaction payments in Carbon Casino cash chips (for sole use within the casino). This currency will then facilitate further profit as it will be gambled in-house. It is here where the largest carbon profit is projected.

Heathrow Carbon Casino Ltd (HCC Ltd) ownership of the facility and all associated airport-based fee-producing assets (with airside tax domicile) provides for a potentially unique business opportunity.

In addition to lower capped rates on carbon trading, airside Carbon Casino Club (CCC) members could be offered further reductions in aircraft fuel costs offset against part-carbon credit levied from casino trading and reducing a percentage of the carbon tax allocated via government fuel duty. Apron aircraft parking costs and car parking could also be reduced, and landing fees could be lowered, encouraging high net worth users to site Heathrow as their priority destination. Therefore, in several key areas the consumer could benefit from being fully immersed in the Carbon Casino experience. ⚏

Note
1. Government moots Personal Carbon Allowance, see www.politics.co.uk/news/domestic-policy/environment/environment/government-moots-personal-carbon-allowance-$445216.htm, accessed 12 October 2007.

Various sections of the Carbon Casino with airside access on the right and landside access on the left.

Cities

As the world has undergone the largest wave of urban growth in human history, is the city slipping out of control? *Geoff Manaugh* paints an emerging picture of metropolitan wildness in which an increasing number of cities become the sites of military conflicts and political, economic and social decay. Could the city be reverting to a medieval model in which illiterate power – criminals, gangs and urban warlords – predominate over rational politics and legitimate government?

Gone Wild

Spencer Murphy, Copehill Down Army Training Enclosure, Shrewton Street, Salisbury Plain, Wiltshire, 2006
Opposite: Copehill Down is a training facility maintained by the Ministry of Defence (MOD) on Salisbury Plain; it is a simulated village in which soldiers plan for the urban warfare of tomorrow. The images here are from Murphy's 'Architects of War' series.

Above: *Playpark.* Surreally, Copehill Down has also hosted the MOD's Grand Challenge, a military robotics competition in which remote-controlled drones are put through strenuous tests.

In the nearly six years since Richard J Norton popularised the term 'feral cities' with his autumn 2003 paper for the *Naval War College Review*, 'Feral Cities: The New Strategic Environment',[1] we have seen Mogadishu, Somalia, become a radiating epicentre of regional sea piracy; we have seen the insurgent city of Fallujah, Iraq, levelled by the US Marine Corps in an operation called 'Phantom Fury'; we have seen a highly infectious disease, SARS, emerge from the densely populated urban agglomerations of southeast China; we have seen the streets of New Orleans filled with troops from the National Guard after the city was all but destroyed by a hurricane; and we have seen the modern city itself revisited as an unkempt site of wilderness, chaos and abandonment in films like *I Am Legend* (2007) and cable television specials such as *Life After People*.

A more amusing example of this trend towards urban wildness comes to us from *The Times*, which reported in November 2008 that: '[m]ost adults think children "are feral and a danger to society"',[2] and that cities like London have become 'infested' with such children, threatening the social fabric itself.

An increasing number of cities, one might say, have gone wild, becoming not centres of vibrant cosmopolitanism, but alarming evidence that the urban world has begun slipping out of control.

An increasing number of cities, one might say, have gone wild, becoming not centres of vibrant cosmopolitanism, but alarming evidence that the urban world has begun slipping out of control. In agreement with a growing number of contemporary urban theorists and geographers, Professor Stephen Graham suggests that this has become, among other things, a situation of utmost military interest. In his forthcoming book *Cities Under Siege: The New Military Urbanism*,[3] Graham writes that: 'Western and Israeli militaries and security forces now perceive all urban terrain as a real or imagined conflict zone inhabited by lurking, shadow enemies, and urban inhabitants as targets that need to be continually tracked, scanned, controlled and targeted.'[4]

This is something Russell W Glenn of the RAND Corporation – an air force think tank based in southern California – calls 'combat in Hell'.[5] In a 1996 report, Glenn pointed out that: 'Urban terrain confronts military

commanders with a synergism of difficulties rarely found in other environments,'[6] many of which are technological. For instance, the effects of radio communications and global positioning systems can be radically limited by dense concentrations of architecture, turning what might otherwise be an exotic experience of pedestrian urbanism into a claustrophobic labyrinth inhabited by enemy combatants. Add to this the fact that military ground operations of the near future are far more likely to unfold in places like Sadr City, Iraq (and not in paragons of city planning like Vancouver), where soldiers will be confronted with an environment in which, as Norton writes, they might be as likely to die from tetanus, rabies and dog attacks as from actual armed combat.[7]

Cities are not just complex administrative challenges, but military problems; seen from this perspective, the city has become a terrifying and unmappable terrain, filled with informal structures, walls, dead ends and narrow alleyways, an environment that must be rethought entirely if seen through the eyes of a war planner or soldier.

In other words, the city still inhabits its historical role as the place to which one goes to find culture, light, music and education. However, the flipside of this is that the city has always been the very site in which one most intensely finds darkness, confrontation and self-erasure. The 'Satanic mills' of Blake, so energetically tackled by 19th-century labour reform and even the public sanitation programmes of early modernity, are still turning.

If there is something new here, though, it is that cities are now where more humans live than ever before, making the species for the first time in its biological history urban, and thus rarely in proximity to something other than itself or its own creations. Indeed, according to the United Nations Population Fund: 'The world is undergoing the largest wave of urban growth in history,'[8] with the result that, by 2008, 'more than half of the world's population [was] living in towns and cities' for the first time.[9] The idea that the city itself could go wild, or even historically backwards, freed from any recognisable stricture of moral standards or 21st-century civility, thus emerges at a particularly interesting moment, the precise moment at which more of us are urban than ever before. If this is the landscape in which we find ourselves now living, then it is only to be expected that cities will also inspire a particularly robust form of nightmarish speculation, becoming not citadels of personal enlightenment but environments of imminent violence, disease, rape, kidnapping, terrorism and death.

It would seem, then, that as the city has become a focus of intense imaginative labour – studied by architects, sociologists, military planners, Hollywood screenwriters and even sci-fi novelists – it has also become a setting for something altogether less utopian than might once have been hoped for in the halcyon days of Modernist social planning. Indeed, as Mike Davis suggests in his book *Planet of Slums*:

The cities of the future, rather than being made out of glass and steel as envisioned by earlier generations of urbanists, are instead largely constructed out of crude brick, straw, recycled plastic, cement blocks, and scrap wood. Instead of cities of light soaring toward heaven, much of the twenty-first-century urban world squats in squalor, surrounded by pollution, excrement, and decay.[10]

Farm. The MOD refers to urban warfare as fighting in built-up areas, or FIBUA (the US equivalent is MOUT – military operations on urban terrain). Acting as if they are in Baghdad, Kabul and even Tehran, soldiers prepare themselves for intense, high-density conflict.

But what is a feral city? Norton himself has some suggestions: 'Imagine a great metropolis covering hundreds of square miles,' he begins.

> Once a vital component in a national economy, this sprawling urban environment is now a vast collection of blighted buildings, an immense petri dish of both ancient and new diseases, a territory where the rule of law has long been replaced by near anarchy in which the only security available is that which is attained through brute power.[11]

With its infrastructure having collapsed long ago – or having never been built in the first place – there are no works of public sanitation, no flood defences, no licensed medical practitioners and no reliable food supply. The feral city is a kind of return to the medieval era, a dark age for anyone but criminals, gangs and urban warlords. It is a time of illiterate power: strength unresponsive to rational politics.

For Norton, feral cities are cities that have failed to deliver on the basic promise of urbanity, failed to live up to the expectations of civilisation itself. The residents have banded together in physical space, only to find that the true enemy from which they must be protected is each other. One might say that this is Nietzsche against Hobbes: that is, these cities have reneged on their promise of a beneficent Leviathan. This new development is as much a problem of philosophy as it is of political theory, and it is rapidly becoming a problem of architecture and urban design. For instance, a feral city's 'buildings, other structures, and subterranean spaces, would offer nearly perfect protection from overhead sensors, whether satellites or unmanned aerial vehicles'.[12] The feral city, that is, is a maze resistant to aerial mapping, its roofscape accessible to surveillance by attack helicopters and Google Earth while its street life remains invisible to organisational oversight. In both legal and visual terms, the feral city is a kind of blind spot: it is, in a literal sense, self-camouflaged.

Unfortunately, and perhaps even because of this, urban ferality also remains understudied. Norton continues:

> Over the past decade or so, a great deal of scholarly attention has been paid to the phenomenon of failing states. In contrast, however, there has been a significant lack of concern for the potential emergence of failed cities.[13]

I would suggest, however, that Norton himself is not immune to this diagnosis; his paper is oddly thin on specifics, describing an environment that sounds rather more like 1980s Brixton and less like the urban 'Hell' of the RAND Corporation. That is, urban ferality would seem to call for a descriptive intensity that Norton's paper ultimately fails to deliver.

At the very least, feral cities are an imaginative resource for writers, film-makers, visual artists and theoreticians – not to mention architects – but Norton's own verbal shaping of these environments somehow fails to inspire true dread. His feral city, in which, he writes, 'social services are all but nonexistent, and the vast majority of the city's occupants have no access to even the most basic health or security assistance',[14] sounds like London during the Thatcher years: dangerous and at risk of infrastructural collapse, but nowhere near the horrific imaginings of contemporary science-fiction novels or even Hollywood thrillers.

These latter genres seem oddly more willing than Norton to imagine the true depravity of an unsupervised urban environment, and this narrative shortcoming is particularly interesting when one recalls that Norton's paper was published by the *Naval War College Review*. Is the military underimagining its own future battlefield? The less than impressive record of the US occupation of Iraq offers its own suggestive answer to this query. What does it mean, then, that films like *28 Days Later* (2002) and *Escape From New York* (1981), novels like Cormac McCarthy's *The Road* (2007) and even early first-person shooter video games such as *Doom* are better than the military at representing the depravities of a landscape gone wild? Should combat theoreticians turn away from their own war college reviews and pick up stacks of comic books, novels and DVDs instead?

I would thus like to propose a research project on the feral city, one that would pass through different historical eras (from the feral towns and plague villages of Europe, after the collapse of the Roman Empire, and the Black Death, to the fire-bombed urban cores of the Second World War), cultural genres (from films like *Assault on Precinct 13* (2005) to novels such as Sol Yurick's *The Warriors* (2003), and from

School. The structures in Copehill Down are red brick and stylistically generic, neither recognisably suburban nor particularly exotic. The village was originally meant to resemble housing in Bavaria.

comic series like Warren Ellis's *Feral City* to video games such as *Warhammer 40,000*), and spatial scales (feral neighbourhoods – even feral buildings – within otherwise functioning cities). It is only when fully considering the range of ferality, so to speak, that we can appreciate how interesting the topic really is and how important it is that these environments given over to chaos can be more accurately examined and described. In its most collaborative form, this could take the shape of an organised research studio dedicated to a study of the wild metropolis, synthesising sci-fi with site visits, anthropological studies of failed cities with cinematic views of those regions' darkest alleyways.

Within any study of ferality, however, there is a continuum of urban wildness that must be explored in far more rigorous detail; after all, if riots, disease and gang warfare are at one end of the feral spectrum, then the unthreatening informality and libertarian quasi-urbanism of summer-camp grounds are at the other.

So where do feral cities stand today? How might we best describe them, or represent them architecturally, in order to study how they came to be created? What does the space of a feral city actually look like? How can it be most effectively mapped? For instance, what is the spatial experience of the feral city for those who live there, and what might an oral history of feral city dwellers tell us about urban life in the 21st century?

Within any study of ferality, however, there is a continuum of urban wildness that must be explored in far more rigorous detail; after all, if riots, disease and gang warfare are at one end of the feral spectrum, then the unthreatening informality and libertarian quasi-urbanism of summer-camp grounds are at the other. Neither of these examples is a centrally administered space of habitation, but at what point does lack of central authority lead to genuine ferality? Further, if a warlord or organised gang is in charge of a certain neighborhood, is that neighborhood truly feral or is it simply subject to a new form of rogue microsovereignty?

This brings us to the unquestioned cultural assumptions that haunt these very questions: whether we are referring to the slums of São Paolo or to the waterfront arms markets of Mogadishu, it is distinctly possible that we use the word 'feral' simply to gloss over the fact that we do not understand how those cities function. Again, this rapidly becomes an architectural concern: we are confronting new types of urban organisation, and new strategies for the inhabitation of the built environment.

Once these questions have been answered, however, will urban planners, city councils and architects be any better at intervening in, and ameliorating, feral cities for their residents? Or would the results of such a study simply be appropriated by the military to organise more effective invasions tomorrow? These are genuine and important research questions and they require a different form of analysis than that presented by Richard J Norton or his intellectual colleagues at the RAND Corporation.

The goal of this research would be to produce a working taxonomy, or descriptive catalogue, of cities gone wild, cutting across genres and historical eras. From Sodom and Gomorrah to the Los Angeles riots, from London's various and ever shifting Murder Miles to the film *Mad Max: Beyond Thunderdome* (1985), by way of Baghdad and Grozny, the feral city is ubiquitous in both history and cultural imagination. Where else might feral cities be discovered – and what spatial or strategic lessons does their existence entail?

As the foreseeable human future becomes more and more thoroughly urbanised, we still have much to learn about how, as a species, we organise ourselves spatially, what potential futures our settled landscapes might hold, and how our relationships to strangers living in close proximity might change under extreme environmental pressures. The limit case of all of this is the feral city. ∆

Notes
1. Richard J Norton, 'Feral Cities', *Naval War College Review*, Autumn 2003, Vol LVI, No 4, pp 97–106.
2. Alexandra Frean, 'Most adults think children "are feral and a danger to society"', *Times Online*, 17 November 2008.
3. Stephen Graham, *Cities Under Siege: The New Military Urbanism*, Verso (London), 2009.
4. Ibid.
5. Russell W Glenn, *Combat in Hell: A Consideration of Constrained Urban Warfare*, RAND Corporation/Arroyo Center National Defense Research Institute (Santa Monica, CA), 1996.
6. Ibid, p viii.
7. For instance, Norton suggests that 'in a combat operation in a feral city the number of casualties from pollutants, toxins, and disease may well be higher than those caused by the enemy.' Norton, op cit, p 105.
8. UNFPA, 'Linking Population, Poverty and Development: Urbanization: A Majority in Cities'. See http://www.unfpa.org/pds/urbanization.htm.
9. Ibid.
10. Mike Davis, *Planet of Slums*, Verso (London), 2006, p 19.
11. Norton, op cit, p 97.
12. Ibid, p 99.
13. Ibid, p 98.
14. Ibid, p 98.

London After

Imagine London amid the ruins, an Arcadian ghost town in which the derelict skyline of Canary Wharf is set in the city's natural landscape of rolling hills. Here **Nic Clear** presents the eerie but strangely beautiful vision that **Ben Marzys** created as the collage storyboards for his film.

Ben Marzys produced his award-winning short film *London After the Rain* while a student in Diploma Unit 15 at the Bartlett School of Architecture. It was the second of his films to be selected by the onedotzero film festival; the first was a short animation made at the beginning of his fourth year and was followed by his final diploma thesis project film *Dystopian Dreams*.

Marzys' film, as the name suggests, references Max Ernst's iconic painting *Europe After the Rain* (1940–2). It presents a strange landscape of rolling hills, junkyards, lagoons and desert outcrops, littered with the 'ruined' fragments of contemporary London. It is a bizarre post-industrial scene, where the city has become largely abandoned and overgrown, though it is still partially

The Rain

Ben Marzys, *London After the Rain*, Diploma Unit 15, Bartlett School of Architecture, UCL, 2007.

inhabited by a strange assortment of humanity accompanied by a variety of unlikely beasts. The film begins with an aircraft bombing one of the empty hillsides and ends with the destruction of the skyscrapers of Canary Wharf. It is melancholy yet intensely beautiful, and consciously references the Arcadian paintings of Claude Lorrain and the compositional ideas and techniques of 'picturesque' landscape design.

Created using a motion-graphic technique in which the layers of the original collage are manipulated to create an apparent depth, the film pans along the landscape, moving in and out of the space. The use of clever transition sequences, where the image of one scene becomes a billboard poster in the next, moves us from one collage to another and gives a sense of hyper-reality and reflexivity to our understanding of the piece.

Presented here is the collage Marzys made as both inspiration and storyboard for the first section of the film. In the collage he maps out the topography of the landscape and organises the events and interventions within the site. Using meticulous collage techniques, he juxtaposed the various elements into an unsettling scenario; although disparate, they are blended together into a seamless, homogeneous spatial construct.

Both drawing and film tap into the contemporary anxieties of economic and environmental collapse, and though the piece is highly playful in its construction and detail, its overall themes are ones of tremendous anxiety and disquiet. ⧄

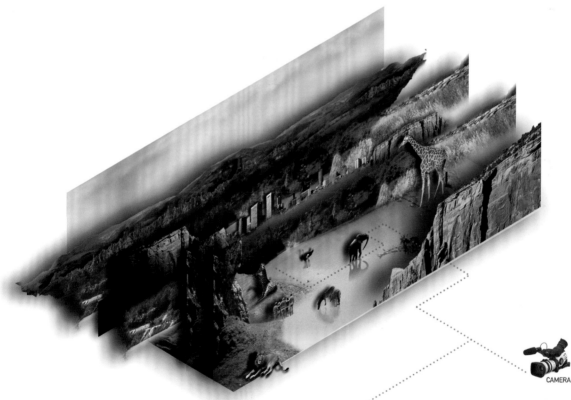

CAMERA

Ben Marzys, *London After the Rain*, Diploma Unit 15,
Bartlett School of Architecture, UCL, 2007.

L.A.W.u.N Project

The project here, begun in 2009 by the Invisible University,[1] a collaboration between the EXP/University of Westminster and the Architectural Association, speculates on the 'dis-urban': new effects on the post-print, post-digital landscape at a local and global level. **Samantha Hardingham and David Greene** provide the narrative.

#21: Cybucolia

The series of three adjusted photographs here are the most up-to-the-minute utterances from the Invisible University, and are direct descendants of *L.A.W.u.N Projects#19: A Book of Provisional Information*[2] and its accompanying exhibition 'L.A.W.u.N Project #20: Imperfect Works', held at the Architectural Association from 28 April to 24 May 2008. In the latest project, invited artists have developed new proposals in response to three of David Greene's past projects that mark strategic moments in moving from Going to the Architecture to Architecture Everywhere: a mosque for Baghdad (1958), Living Pod (1964) and The World's Last Hardware Event (1967). The three tableaux and their accompanying descriptions uncover an opportunity to delve into the depths of the hidden potential atmospheres alluded to by the models that stood in the exhibition, when such imaginings were not yet prepared to be conjured.

Rome-worship in Britain was such that Romans by 1730 were saying: 'Were our amphitheatre portable, the English would carry it off.'
EW Manwaring, *Italian Landscape in Eighteenth Century England*, 1925[3]

Notes
1. L.A.W.u.N Project #21 is a collaboration between David Greene, Samantha Hardingham, Rowan Mersh, Theo Spyropoulos, Shin Egishira, Isabel Peripherique, Edwin Kendall, Kevin Shepherd and Sara Shafiei.
2. David Greene and Samantha Hardingham, *L.A.W.u.N Projects#19: A Book of Provisional Information*, Architectural Association (London), 2008.
3. EW Manwaring, *Italian Landscape in Eighteenth Century England*, Cass (London), 1925.

Itinerant battery-powered coastal terrain
Digital print, 54 layers, 6614 x 4331 pixels
Stupefied by the micro-sequins of a postdigital construction site revisited, almost anything that you can imagine is going to happen. Radically altered sociocultural investigations into conditions of an architecture as a sensitive responsive system, an electronic topology constantly tuning and retuning itself. The cool metallic scaffolds move by toppling over (a very reliable way to get around) and crane armatures lean into the lightness of night-time, assembling and reassembling a superbly eloquent but broken architecture. Wrecked urbanity upon wrecked urbanity, dainty weeds, mouldering aqueducts, unseen larks disturbing the rumble of construction. The scanty antiquarian remnants of Living Pod move in a romantic reverie towards a soft, placid, essentially innocent present to the peaceful bleating of sheep.

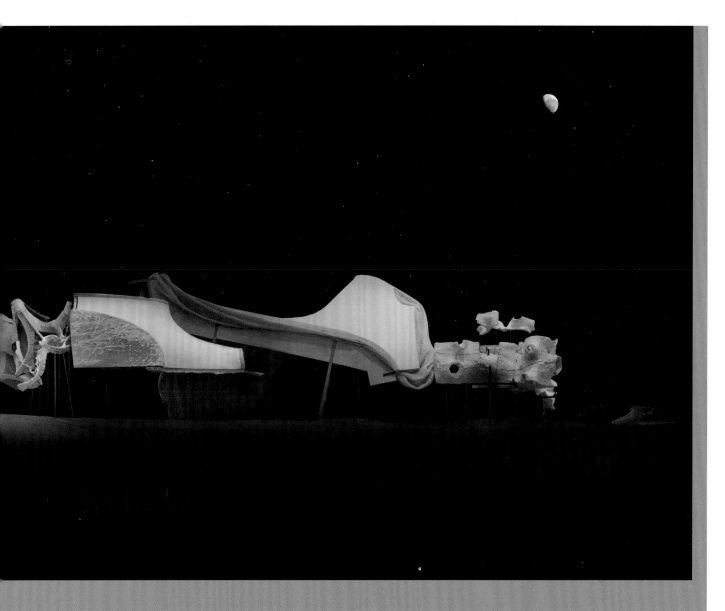

A well-serviced primitive explores the architecture of the New Nature
Digital print, 36 layers, 2481 x 3424 pixels

opposite: This pastoral scene belongs to a series of adjusted photographs that take the atmospheric effects associated with the Invisible University and bring them to an out-into-the-open spatial ambience. For the nomad in the foreground there is neither interior nor exterior: clothed in electro-social camouflage she dissolves into the ravine, gazing into its luminous, mist air while learning the line and musing on the unique phenomena of distance versus memory. Who knew that wet-look, high-tech, liquid-crystal filaments would find a soul mate in a constellation of knitted stretch jersey, constricting and expanding with each movement faster and everywhere, closer to the sky and further from the ground, save for a shadow flung by a passing cloud.

Heavens! Thought I to myself, how times are changed
Digital print, 111 layers, 6614 x 4331 pixels

above: Being susceptible to the delicious disease, Near Future *Ruinenstimmung* necessitates a return to the unfinished detail of what may have been a mosque. A tottering edifice resists the impending silt of dreary sand, shells and expansion mousse. The hermit has died. Having visited a decade previously, the nomad spent much time with a melancholy delight in taking a prospect of its completion. Now, by making four segments in gypsum and clay, it is just enough to imagine the rest. 'I am modelling them in order to appropriate everything.' She stayed to gaze and reflect on both the moribund state of her finances and the illusory nature of buried treasure. There is the essence of ruin-magic. ∆D

Cortical

Could the near future for architects all be in the mind? With further neurological metamorphosis, **Dan Farmer** suggests that spatial awareness and experience could be stipulated by cortical plasticity, stimulated by electrical impulses. With this shift to internalised space perception, the disciplines of architecture and cognitive science become blurred as the relationship between the object and its environment dissolves.

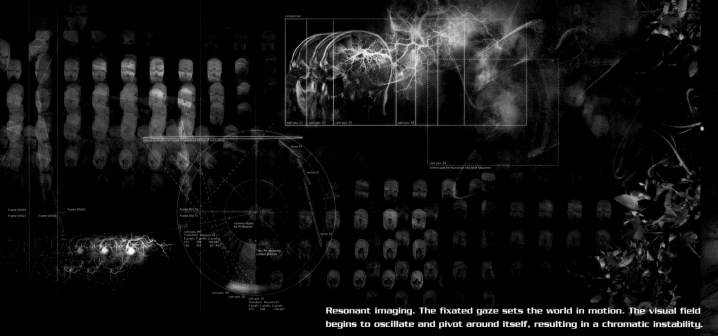

Resonant imaging. The fixated gaze sets the world in motion. The visual field begins to oscillate and pivot around itself, resulting in a chromatic instability.

Plasticity

Scene analysis from *Synaptic Landscapes*. 'My visual cortex has pick... acuity ... it is controlled locally. Visual space will now be my own co...

Changes in the characteristics of matter – a metamorphosis, a transition into an alternative state of mind, independent of our external worlds.

object of parallax. 'This world can be truly inhabited, constructed between my personal fact and fable.'

One must construct a spatial field of objects starting from basic principles, without the hindrance of previous experience. The body, in turn, acts as a semionaut recording edges, gradient and frequencies. Film still from *Synaptic Landscapes*.

Cyto-architecture. Nerves, as the devices of perception, are not interested in light. Nerves only care for geometry, they are stimulated by borders, boundaries, edges and angles. Film still from *Synaptic Landscapes*.

Technology and architecture have become synonymous. Digital media has become paramount in the practice of architecture, specifically within the context of architectural representation. Consequently, how we design, perceive and experience spatial boundaries has altered. Film production, as a time-based medium, grasps the potential to explore new possibilities of architectural representation and practice within a filmic experience. Since the beginning of the 19th century we have assumed that vision can be explained as a two-dimensional image projected on to the back of the retina, and architectural representation has followed this dogma. Cognitive science has progressed. So too must our concept of architectural representation. It is no longer enough to accept a two-dimensional image as a true representation of the environment that we physically occupy.

The realm of cognitive science can be seen as a discipline that inherently deals with the virtuality of self and one's environment far beyond that of line drawings, fly-throughs and digital models. We should look to prominent neurologist Oliver Sack's definition of the brain, specifically the visual system, as being dynamic and active, and perhaps more importantly malleable and adaptive, desperately seeking a coherent self.[1] The two realms of mind and matter are inextricably linked and belong to one another. The brain autonomously constructs its own sense of self and world. We are on the cusp of a neurological metamorphosis, stipulated by the rules of cortical plasticity. Any change in the cortical order of the visual cortex will, in turn, have a direct effect on the mental order. Experienced self and space will become reduced to electrical pulses.

We now need to look to the rules that guide this 'dynamism' of the visual cortex, not the relationship between an object and its environment. Space perception becomes internalised. As the disciplines of architecture and cognitive science become blurred, vision, for architects, cannot be based solely on either localisationist or holistic theories – but rather on one of experience.

The cartographer. All fleeting impressions are briefly recorded in new configurations. This framework creates a constantly changing internal environment. Film still from *Synaptic Landscapes.*

The solipsistic mirror. When the environment becomes one with the internal, the self is found.

The disconnected shot. Only when one narrows in on specific areas of the visual field does its strangeness, or the complex relations of one part of it to another, become apparent.

The synaptic framework. Here, now, these spatial representations are temporal, dynamic and continuously updated, definable solely as interesting correlations, the forms of neural networks. Film still from *Synaptic Landscapes*.

We need to accept that objects in the 'real' world do not project their inherent colours on to our retinal cells. Our perception of colour is based on a combination of wavelength – short/blue, middle/green, long/red. A synaptic connection transfers the stimulus from the retinal cells on to the bipolar cells, which in turn transfer the stimulus on to the ganglion cells and into the optic nerve. Once we as architects are able to choose which neurons are stimulated, diverting them from well-worn neural paths, we can dictate the nature of our surroundings. By manipulating the visual process, entire environments can be constructed and fully experienced, yet be free from physical location: a 'synaptic landscape' where each manipulation creates a different space from one individual to another based on their discrete personal experience.

The brain is not preprogrammed and static – the camera analogy no longer applies – and the visual cortex is not merely a lens but a seeker of rational truth, open to injury and error. Synaptic landscapes can be truly inhabited, constructed between the auteur's personal fact and fable. Perhaps everyone can now become their own architect and director, capable of recreating and inhabiting their own environments within the internal networks of their cortical orders. The same configuration of networks may be stimulated from person to person, yet each representation will inevitably remain completely unique due to the individual's past experience. Architectural representation has now moved away from intricate line drawings printed on paper, or three-dimensional digital (or physical) models, to consist of complex configurations within one's own cyto-architecture. ∆

The synaptic landscape: a battle between planes amid a web of internal spatial geometries.

Note
1. Oliver Sacks, *An Anthropologist On Mars*, Picador (London), 1995, p xv.

The Ridiculous and the Sublime

Ben Nicholson's classic satire *The World Who Wants It?* was written at the beginning of this decade in the wake of 9/11. Here Nicholson revisits the work, presenting new drawings and rethinking the themes in light of the second major hit that the world has taken with the banking crisis of 2008 and the accompanying economic downturn.

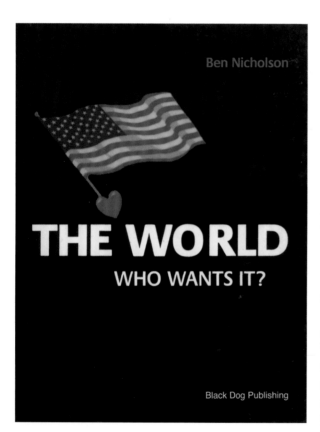

The World Who Wants It?
A satire on the ethics of green politics in America, including scores of can-do projects to realign its moral fibre. The book concludes with a plan to spend $20 billion on rebuilding Old Jerusalem, in a way that just might make sense.

When the rivers of money run dry and governments start to focus less on jobs and volunteerism and more on preventing their citizens from revolting, a few things can still be done in the discipline of architecture (apart from the obvious: ie, a roof, warmth and food).

At one end of the spectrum the world's wrongs can be seen for what they are and set on course by writing. To this end the satire *The World Who Wants It?* was begun on 12 September 2001, the chilly morning after 9/11.[1]

Simultaneously, a spatial practice was initiated that bypassed the building industry entirely, instead choreographing a way of walking and looking and doing without recourse to matter. Life in a Supermax prison was imagined, a place where neon light is left burning 24/7 and there is nothing sharp (like a pencil) with which to while away the days. What could be done with the body in a place like that, to keep the mind alive? In response to this eventuality, a project was begun to draw out a taxonomy of hundreds of labyrinths. The labyrinth is the most essential fixed spatial construct known in architecture, save standing still on terra firma.

Architectural Restitution
Writing satire offers the chance to imagine a way to visualise the world's wrongs and set them right through a method that is as absurd as it is honest. After *The World Who Wants It?* was written, the status quo of the world has wobbled and has taken a second major hit with the credit crunch meltdown. Curiously, the ideas in the satire are beginning to make sense, and some scenarios are playing out in real time, sort of. It seems that the West is now open to systemic change. Now that human beings are no longer effective consumers or even producers, what are we going to do to make life meaningful, and what will happen to the architectural machine that has supported the consumptive way of life for so long? In essence, the American interpretation of 'saving energy' was to have the same way of life at half the price, but now there is the possibility for 'behaviour change'. It is this aspect of change that architecture is especially adaptive towards, and where real restitution can take place.

God Bless America

There is no doubt that America's hubris and quest of the soft life has been its undoing. My great, great grandmother was buried in Lucknow during the Indian Mutiny, also known as the Great Rebellion of 1857, so I know first-hand the consequences of *la dolce vita* and the miscreant imperialism that supports it. After 9/11, GOD BLESS AMERICA buttons were on every American's lapel, but the punctuation was all wrong. During the Bush years the buttons could have carried the slightly stronger exhortation GOD: BLESS AMERICA. Now, in the Obama years, the buttons might promote a more buoyant GOD BLESS! AMERICA.

Sugar Man and Whipping Boy

In the first part of the mission set forth in *The World Who Wants It?*, moral turpitude is confronted. An initiative is put in motion to mirror America's Peace Corps Program with a newly formed Bilateral Peace Corps (BPC). BPC workers come from all over the world to help America in its time of need. To tackle overeating, Tibetan Sherpas provide their services by carrying a stack of 5-pound (2.3-kilogram) bags of sugar on their backs, the total weight equalling the pounds that an individual needs to lose. The designated whipping boy follows the weight watcher around and, as he or she loses 5 pounds, the Sherpa dumps a bag of sugar. In this way we see the consequences of our actions. Sooner or later the Sherpa and the American will have shed their loads, will stand up straight and be able to look each other squarely in the eye. The Sherpa gets paid off with a tidy remittance and the individual with an eating problem is now buff: everyone is happy.

Clothing and Beauty

In essence, a well-appointed SUV is a steel burka, a place in which one is protected from the hurly-burly of life and all the unwanted attentions that it brings, yet with just enough clues to maintain an aura of sex appeal. The concept of individual, lightweight, 100 per cent green, go-anywhere protection in the form of a burka might be just what the West is looking for. What would happen if a contestant in a beauty pageant turned up in a burka? Would this be the sign that the West's infatuation with bare skin had changed into an infatuation with subtle nuance?

Sugar Man and Whipping Boy
Overeaters are provided with Tibetan Sherpas to carry 5-pound (2.3-kilogram) bags of sugar, equal to the pounds a weight-watcher wishes to lose. When the dieter loses 5 pounds, the Sherpa dumps a bag of sugar, thus making visible the weight problem at hand, as well as the pain and suffering.

Miss Wisconsin goes burka!
In an age of monitoring sex to new degrees, the concept of an individual, lightweight, 100 per cent green, go-anywhere emotional prophylactic in the form of a burka might be just what the West desires. What would happen if a beauty pageant contestant turned up in a burka?

The Rock of Sakhra: a spinning axis mundi
For millennia, Jews, Christians and Muslims have fixated on a single large rock atop Mount Moriah in Jerusalem. It is the world's most important real estate bar none. New air nozzles spin the rock at breakneck speed, engineering our axis mundi to spread its powers without prejudice.

America liberates Jerusalem
10,000 peacekeepers liberate Jerusalem, creating an otherworldly city free of politics. The peacekeepers distribute $200 billion to relocate the Israeli and Palestinian capitals to Tel Aviv and Ramallah respectively, and go on to build a new temple, cathedral and mosque in the New Jerusalem.

Heaven on Earth: Jerusalem

It is not fully appreciated that the current 'Middle East Crisis' has a great deal to do with landscape and architecture. The Crusades, Bush's oil wars and the intifadas are spatial foreplay for the real point of contention: the Rock of Sakhra. On the top of Mount Moriah in Jerusalem rests a large rock that has had a varied history, depending on whom you talk to. The Jews believe that Abraham was about to sacrifice Isaac on this rock. The Christians believe that the chunk removed from it held the Ark of the Covenant and the Holy Grail, thought to now be in Rosslyn, Scotland. The Muslims believe the rock to be the base of a 12,000-cubit column reaching to heaven, which Muhammad climbed when visiting the prophets on his 'night journey'. Today the Dome of the Rock is in the cross hairs of every itchy-fingered fundamentalist slinging an RPG-7 or GBU-28. Tomorrow the rock could release its status of being the solitary axis mundi by being set spinning in perpetual motion every which way by hi-tech air jets: a political solution morphs into a sculptural solution.

Aedificare delequare

From the dawn of time, superpowers west of the Euphrates marshes have been obliged to take on the task of looking after Jerusalem during their tenure. In a bold move, America steps up to the plate and creates a spectacular show of its airpower above the Holy City, out of which tumble 10,000 paratrooping peacekeepers. The peacekeepers, all of whom are freemasons of a high order, wear helmets emblazoned with the words *aedificare delequare*: TO BUILD AND TO DESTROY. The sitting president sets up a special $200 billion fund to rebuild the Holy City, moving the secular capitals of Israel and Palestine to Tel Aviv and Ramallah respectively. The New Jerusalem becomes an otherworldly city, free of politics and reserved for the triune of Abrahamic religions with a new temple, cathedral and mosque, the likes of which the world has not yet seen. Making three stunning buildings and their associative infrastructure is deemed to be cheaper than conducting another war. An architectural solution has been made for a political pickle, which gives the respective congregations exactly what they hanker after.

American peacekeeper

All the peacekeepers are freemasons selected from a high order. Their helmets sport a decal with the words *aedificare delequare*: to build and to destroy beneath which is a bush surmounting two crossed matches, one normal and the other safety, representing resolve and restraint.

A Kentucky festival of machine guns

A semiannual festival of machine guns is held in Kentucky to test their owners' mettle. For some, this is the epicentre of political incorrectness and for others a God-given portal to freedom. The landscape of Knob Creek is a site of unprecedented power, the earth pierced with excruciating care and abandon.

Guns and Butter

Each year, at the Knob Creek Gun Range at Fort Knox, a festival of machine guns takes place in the spring and fall. Approximately 120,000 civilian licenses for machine guns are in circulation in the US, and the semi-annual Knob Creek event is the epicentre of this blip on the politically incorrect landscape. America is a place of extraordinary paradoxes, and the rich conflicts associated with guns and butter reach all the way to the geometer's table. While I was researching eighth-century Greek geometric vases, the four-limbed spiral (aka swastika) kept popping up, to the degree that progress could not be made without its acknowledgement. Having fled to geometry, as the de facto language of non-political gesture, I found myself once more entering design taboo. Who in their right mind would decorate a wall with swastikas; but then who in their right mind would be party to expunging one of the most beautiful forms in decorative history, just because of a bunch of Nazis?

A wall of four-limbed spirals

Researching the taxonomy of Greek vase decoration inevitably leads to the four-limbed spiral, aka the swastika. To address the design taboo against swastikas, one of the most significant forms in design, a wall of spirals is built out of Kufi blocks in Peter Eisenmann's DAAP Building in Cincinnati.

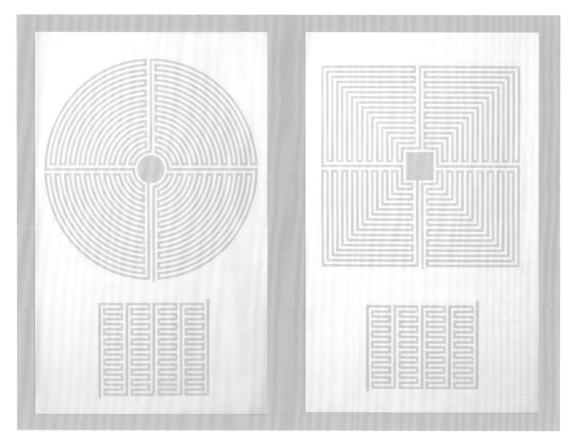

Roman labyrinths: the masters of spatial repetition
The Romans were the masters of spatial repetition; communication meant straight roads and level viaducts contoured around hills. The meditative constructs they made were equally clean; simple back-and-forth reciprocations arranged in squares and circles – labyrinths maybe, journeys into the underlying psyche more probable.

Restitution: Engaging Architecture's Sixth Sense

In a search for a practice of design that is beyond both 'green' and 'taboo', where on earth can one look: inward? Does the energy leaking from the pineal gland detect spatial qualities that are traditionally invisible? How do we design for the intangible, where the white space that surrounds architecture is sensed? Maybe the hyper-cycle of making stuff and building buildings will lead to a resurgent interest in the ineffable, ushering in a wholesale rejection of matter. Could this be our 'ghost dance' moment, when the ethereal engages the visceral to make a sublime construct of nothingness?

What is the equivalent word to 'go walkabout'? Is it 'wandering' or 'wanderlust' or maybe 'meandering'? If humans were spiders, paying out a silken thread wherever they went, they would find that each person's passage on earth is nothing more than a single line. We like to think that one foot goes one place and the imagination takes the other somewhere else. But no, everyone walks a continuous line through life – no ifs, ands or buts.

A labyrinth is a raw architectural plan without substance, save the invitation to walk in dust. It sets in motion an intermingling of people, where the backs of hands brush against each other and the body pivots on a heel to confront someone face to face. At one moment you are held enveloped by others; the tables then turn and it is you who does the holding.

With each visit to a labyrinth an exfoliation of energy is shed, building a repository in the ground that accumulates incrementally to make a fund of something that lingers. The more wellbeing that is left in any place, the more it can give to those who leave in its bosom their hurt. Yet places can be worn down by giving too much – a battlefield, for example. Cities becomes rich when they accumulate the collective energy left there, be this from animals or humankind. Surely that is why some fields still sing long after the memory of what once happened there has dissolved.

Enacting architecture can be done without building. By engaging the ground in the most direct way with the least possible means, spatial constructs are formed that give flight to fancy, and can be passed on to others with a simple nod and a spring in the foot. **Δ**

Note
1. Ben Nicholson, *The World Who Wants It?*, Black Dog Press (London), 2004.

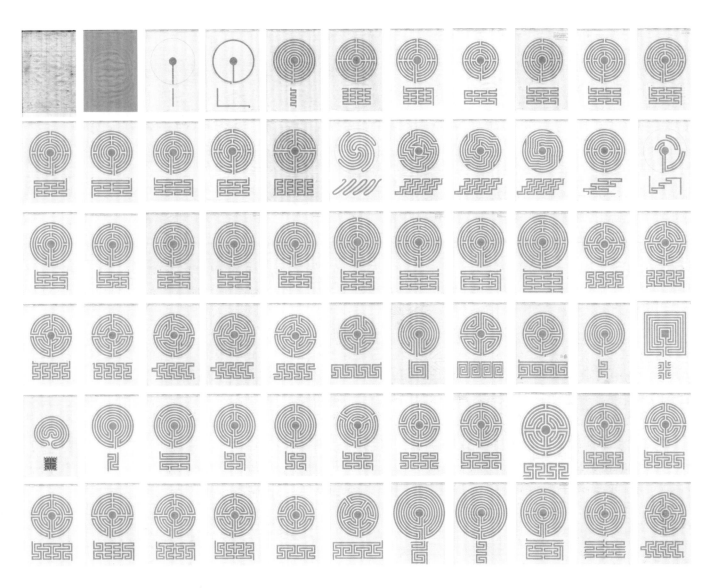

Taxonomy of small labyrinths

above: About 70 designs for labyrinths have been used since antiquity. A simple rotating tile can generate thousands of designs, the majority genetic chaff, but those that strain out choreograph essential body movements of serpentine turns, staggering, meandering, mirroring and spiralling – not much else is needed.

Shuffle labyrinth, Whitewater, New Mexico

left: On the edge of the Gila Wilderness, a disc of laterite soil is dug free of plants, inviting humans to shuffle their feet in mud or dust. Labyrinth designs are committed to memory, or intuited, and drawn out in footprints. They create the most direct architectural plans known, and are always open to change.

Stereoscopic Urbanism

JG Ballard and the Built Environment

Michelle Lord, Future Ruins (inspired by JG Ballard's 'The Ultimate City'), 2008
'Pulled apart by the elders, many of the sets revealed their internal wiring. The green and yellow circuitry, the blue capacitors and modulators, mingled with the bright berries of the firethorn, rival orders of a wayward nature merging again after millions of years of separate evolution.' JG Ballard, 'The Ultimate City', 1976.

*The fiction of JG Ballard was centred almost wholly on the built environment. Ballard took architectural design to its logical extreme and then contorted it further. **Simon Sellars** looks at how architects can learn from Ballard and, specifically, his use of urban sound as a metaphor.*

In JG Ballard's 'The Sound-Sweep',[1] the sonic strata of everyday urban life – a 'frenzied hypermanic babel of jostling horns, shrilling tyres, plunging brakes and engines'[2] – is so without respite that it is literally embedded within walls and surfaces and must be vacuumed away with a device called the 'sonovac'. The central character, Mangon, is a mute who has developed hyperacute hearing, making him a valued sound-sweep. His main client is Madame Gioconda, an ex-opera singer whose career ended with the advent of 'ultrasonic music'. Ultrasonic producers electronically rescore classical symphonies into musical notation that operates on a subliminal level, making use of the sensorium beyond the normal range of the human ear. Supposedly the new music, ostensibly silent, has richer texture, theme and emotion, but whether this is merely a placebo effect to placate the frazzled masses remains ambiguous.

Mangon strives to resurrect Gioconda's career, but when he does eventually stage her comeback, she botches it, her voice so cracked, out of practice and out of tune that it causes great distress to all who hear it. The story ends with Mangon driving off in his sound truck as he turns on the vehicle's inbuilt sonovac – filled with the city's sonic detritus – to drown out Gioconda singing like an 'insane banshee'. Effectively, Mangon manipulates the sounds of the city to assuage his psychological turmoil.

Ballard's story anticipates R Murray Schafer's World Soundscape project, which aimed to reduce the noise pollution of industrial environments in favour of an 'acoustic ecology', eliminating so-called 'bad' sounds in favour of prescribed 'good' sounds, returning to 'the Ursound' supposedly found in nature, where, Schafer rhapsodises, 'listening blindly to our ancestors and the wild creatures, we will feel it surge within us again, in our speaking and in our music'.[3] But as Geoff Manaugh notes:

> Where the Project went wrong … was when it thought it had a kind of sonic monopoly over what sounded good. Industrial noises would be scrubbed from the city … and a nostalgic calm … infused in its place. Think church bells, not automobiles. But where would such sensory cleansing leave those … who enjoy the sounds of factories?[4]

'Halloway had the distinct impression that this solitary young mute was a prisoner here, high above this museum of cars in the centre of the abandoned airport.' JG Ballard, 'The Ultimate City', 1976.

For Ballard, too, neither full reliance on technology (represented by the sterile, calming aesthetic of ultrasonic music) nor the reactionary turn to nostalgia and a safe retreat into the past (ie Mangon's initial deification of the opera singer) is posited as an adequate solution. Instead, a middle ground is sought, a strategy found throughout his career, grounded in the sense that the built environment must be met on its own terms.

In the novella 'The Ultimate City',[5] Ballard moves beyond Mangon's half-aware thumbnail sketch and into a three-dimensionality: a full-scale cognitive remapping. A future ecotopia, Garden City, has developed wind power and alternative technologies after New York has fallen into ruins from the exhaustion of fossil fuels. The central character, Halloway, dissatisfied with what he sees as the dulling of the imagination in Garden City, with its organic conformity, makes his way back to the abandoned New York, where he attempts to restart the metropolis and its power supplies. Significantly, it is the noise of the city that he misses and that he is inescapably drawn to. With the help of Olds (another mute), Halloway manages to

restart the generators and power supplies of a small sector of the city, bringing to life neon and traffic lights, while broadcasting sound-effects records of automobile and aircraft noise:

Halloway moved from one apartment to the next, flicking lights on and off, working the appliances in the kitchens. Mixers chattered, toasters and refrigerators hummed, warning lights glowed in control panels ... Television sets came on, radios emitted a ghostly tonelessness interrupted now and then by static from the remote-controlled switching units of the tidal pumps twenty miles away.

It was only now, in this raucous light and noise, that the city was being its true self, only in this flood of cheap neon that it was really alive ....[6]

Like Mangon, but on a grander scale, Halloway tunes the city rather than shutting it out, rejecting the sterile, affectless Garden City for a complete reimagining and re-envisaging of the city's technological grid, including the acoustic footprint that so disturbed the inventors of ultrasonic music. This time, the story anticipates the Positive Soundscapes research project, funded by the Engineering and Physical Sciences

Research Council and comprising five British universities, which aims to convince architects and town planners to think beyond the traditional focus on reducing noise levels and to pay attention instead to 'the many possibilities for creating positive environments in the soundscapes in which we live. People can completely change their perception of a sound once they have identified it. In the laboratory, many listeners prefer distant motorway noise to rushing water, until they are told what the sounds are.'[7]

I have cited these examples of urban sound in Ballard because they represent the key components of a framework he uses to critique the psychological and perceptual dimensions that are saturated in the built environment, but that seem lacking in the discourse that generates architectural practice. In a sense, Ballard's work is about nothing but the built environment. It is often said that technology and the liminal zones of suburbia and non-place urban fields are his main characters, and indeed the buildings and zones he erects – the motorway system in *Crash*,[8] the apartment block in *High-Rise* ('an environment built, not for man, but for man's absence'),[9] the secessionist shopping centre in *Kingdom Come*[10] – all

'Buckmaster tried to point out to Halloway how the Twentieth Century had met its self-made death. They stood on the shores of artificial lagoons filled with chemical wastes, drove along canals silvered by metallic scum, across landscapes covered by thousands of tons of untreated garbage, fields piled high with cans, broken glass and derelict machinery.' JG Ballard, 'The Ultimate City', 1976.

seem imbued with an artificial intelligence determined to eradicate human life as if it were a disease.

This is a gambit that brings sociologist Ron Smith's observation into stark relief: 'If you want to see what's wrong with architecture today, pick up the latest issue of almost any architectural design magazine. They're filled with pictures of interesting architecture, but you rarely see any people actually using those buildings.'[11] In Ballard, trends (and flaws) in architectural design are pursued to their logical extremes, and then bent backwards or forwards through time to go completely beyond logic. In the real world, people might complain about an escalator too far away from a baggage chute in an airport or a concourse in a mall that heats up too quickly, or overly processed floors that make far too much noise when walked upon. In Ballard, the unspoken tension and psychopathology engendered by such scenarios is recycled, reheated and allowed free rein to play itself out to the bitterest of ends.

In **High-Rise**, *which charts the breakdown of the social order in a neo-Corbusian residential building, at first it is the little things that niggle. These then overlay and overlap, each new escalation of hostilities a clear and logical progression from the previous strata, however bizarre each incident might seem in isolation.*

In *High-Rise*, which charts the breakdown of the social order in a neo-Corbusian residential building, at first it is the little things that niggle. These then overlay and overlap, each new escalation of hostilities a clear and logical progression from the previous strata, however bizarre each incident might seem in isolation. Parents find that the building hasn't been designed for children: there is no free, open space, only 'someone else's car park'. Shared garbage disposal causes anxiety and division between residents. Raucous parties occur on the upper floors, and residents in 'better-sited apartments' are unsympathetic to those living below them. Dog owners are attacked for allowing their pets to urinate and defecate in the elevators, culminating in the fateful moment when one resident's Afghan hound is drowned in the swimming pool.

Thereafter, things really take off: incidents of violent aggression morph into tribal skirmishes and warring groups cut off escalator access, barricading their apartments and 'Balkanising' the middle section of flats to form a buffer zone. Yet, after the system has collapsed and failed, what we are left with is more than a mere glimmer of hope, and clearly akin to a programme of resistance based on emergent psychologies and a radical new approach to the built environment: 'Even the run-down nature of the high-rise was a model of the world into which the future was carrying them, a landscape beyond technology where everything was either derelict or, more ambiguously, recombined in unexpected but more meaningful ways.'[12]

'[But] Halloway was fascinated by the glimmering sheen of the metal-scummed canals, by the strange submarine melancholy of drowned cars looming up at him from abandoned lakes, by the brilliant colours of the garbage hills, by the glitter of a million cans embedded in a matrix of detergent packs and tinfoil, a kaleidoscope of everything they could wear, eat and drink.' JG Ballard, 'The Ultimate City', 1976.

Yet just as Positive Soundscapes has encountered resistance in persuading architects and engineers to re-evaluate environmental sound, 'perhaps because of barriers to communication across different disciplines'[13] chances are you will not find Ballard on the syllabus. According to Nic Clear, who has used Ballard's work as an aid in architectural learning: 'Within academia and architectural criticism, if such a thing still exists, there is a general disdain for "popular" fiction – writing on, and about, architecture is still very elitist – and I have met quite a bit of resistance when discussing Ballard as a serious subject.'[14]

Yet architects have no compunction about appropriating critical theory to their own ends. Peter Eisenman drew heavily on Deleuze and Baudrillard for his conception of 'interstitial' architecture and 'blurred zones', where the aim was to examine the way the virtual has invaded the actual, displacing architecture's traditional role as an anchor for the real. Eisenman's 'philosophy lite' sought to invite architecture to explore conceptual spaces located within the 'folds' of the built environment, with the aim of 'refram[ing] existing urbanism, to set it off in a new direction'.[15] But surely the theory of Deleuze (which has more than a few correspondences with the work of Ballard) is designed to inspire affirmation in the reader, the user, the inhabitant; surely it must be tangible and must work in practice, in real-world terms, in that it must inspire thought and positive action to affirm its validity.

That to me seems the Deleuzian ideal – indeed, the Ballardian ideal. It would seem apposite to say the majority of criticism of Eisenman's buildings implies that not only are most users unaware of the inner workings of the 'process of the interstitial' that built the thing, but that in the final product antagonism and negation is placed before affirmation and interaction. As Roger Kimball writes:

> When we encounter a stairway that leads nowhere … we need [Eisenman's] help to understand that we are being given a lesson in linguistic futility. Otherwise we might foolishly conclude that it was just a stairway that led nowhere and wonder about the sanity of the chap who paid the architect's bill.[16]

The psychological dimension of urban life plays an important part, 'reading' and 'writing' the city on a sensory level.

Ballard is interested in urbanism and spatial dynamics as a way to understand the city as narrative. The psychological dimension of urban life plays an important part, 'reading' and 'writing' the city on a sensory level. Indeed, he should be required reading for anyone seriously interested in making architecture more 'user friendly', or to anyone who thinks that architecture should be more than a series of shiny icons designed by remote starchitects. In this, he is ideally matched with the aims of Smith, who believes that 'to become truly great architects [architecture students] also have to be great social psychologists, community sociologists, and organizational theorists',[17] and also those of Michael Kroelinger, who teaches a course in 'Architectural Sociology' at the University of Nevada that 'underscores the importance of understanding people's values, needs, and attitudes, from an individual level to an organizational one'.[18]

Architects: read, study and learn from Ballard's writing. Because it should not be the job of the architect to build worlds and indulge the luxury of allowing them to fail at our expense, but that of the writer, the constructor of virtual worlds that live, breathe and, indeed, die in virtuality so that we, in the actual, do not have to expire to prove a point. Only then should we overlay the virtual with the actual to create a stereoscopic representation, a truly interstitial process that places the user at the centre with the power to inform, direct, stage and manage the terms of his or her movement through time and space, perhaps nudging us one step closer to a read/write city in which we are free to 'tune' the built environment,[19] free to contribute to the conditions of our cohabitation.

In fact, an interdisciplinary, specifically Ballardian approach may be exactly what is required to shake architecture out of its 'business as usual' mentality, forcing it to confront the global economic and environmental crises just over the horizon. Ask the question: is another 'shiny, happy' building really what we want or need to see or inhabit? Δ

'He knew now that he would never return to Garden City, with its pastoral calm ... he would set off on foot, ... following the memorials westwards across the continent, until he found the old man again and could help him raise his pyramids of washing machines, radiator-grilles and typewriters.' JG Ballard, 'The Ultimate City', 1976.

Notes

1. JG Ballard, 'The Sound-Sweep' [1960], in *The Complete Short Stories*, Flamingo (London), 2001.

2. Ibid, p 106.

3. Quoted in Brandon LaBelle, *Perspectives on Sound Art*, Continuum (New York and London), 2006, p 204.

4. Geoff Manaugh, 'Audio Architecture', *BLDGBLOG*, 10 August 2007. See http://bldgblog.blogspot.com/2007/08/audio-architecture.html, accessed 26 January 2008.

5. JG Ballard, 'The Ultimate City' [1976], in *The Complete Short Stories*, Flamingo (London), 2001.

6. Ibid, pp 902, 907.

7. Positive Soundscapes, 'Project Overview', *Positive Soundscapes: A Re-evaluation of Environmental Sound*. See www.positivesoundscapes.org/project_overview, accessed 26 January 2009.

8. JG Ballard, *Crash* [1973], Vintage (London), 1995.

9. JG Ballard, *High-Rise* [1975], Flamingo (London), 1993.

10. JG Ballard, *Kingdom Come*, Fourth Estate (London), 2006.

11. Quoted in Gian Galassi, 'Community by Design', *UNLV Magazine*, Fall 2004. See http://magazine.unlv.edu/Issues/Fall04/community.html>, accessed 26 January 2009.

12. JG Ballard, *High Rise*, op cit, p 147.

13. Positive Soundscapes, op cit.

14. Simon Sellars, 'Architectures of the Near Future: An Interview with Nic Clear', *Ballardian*, 24 December 2008. See www.ballardian.com/near-future-nic-clear-interview, accessed 26 January 2009.

15. Peter Eisenman (ed), *Blurred Zones: Investigations of the Interstitial: Eisenman Architects 1988–1998*, Monacelli Press (New York), 2002, p 132.

16. Roger Kimball, 'Architecture and ideology', *New Criterion*, December 2002. See http://findarticles.com/p/articles/mi_hb3345/is_4_21/ai_n28962509>, accessed 26 January 2009.

17. Quoted in Gian Galassi, op cit.

18. Ibid.

19. I've borrowed the concept of the 'read/write' city from Steve Lambert of the Anti-Advertising Agency who, writing about the visual environment and street art, states: 'Why is read/write better? Because you can consume, process, and respond. This is how we think critically. This is how we learn. You can talk back. You can express yourself. You don't just consume expression, you create expression. Read/write is how democracy works. There's a reason kids want to write their names on walls. There's a reason why people take graffiti seriously. Granted, graffiti writers don't always know how to direct this energy, but I'd argue there's some overlap with the reasons one writes their name on a wall and the reasons one runs for the school board. Being able to write means being able to affect your environment. To change it. You exist in the world not as a consumer, but an active citizen. Read only culture creates apathy.' From Steve Lambert, 'Demand a Read/Write City', *The Anti-Advertising Agency*, 3 October, 2008. See http://antiadvertisingagency.com/news/demand-a-readwrite-city, accessed 26 January 2009.

THE SOUND

For **George Thomson**, JG Ballard's 1960 short story 'The Sound-Sweep' provided the essential springboard for a short animated film centred around the M25 and Bluewater. The super-regional shopping centre is transformed, after a series of targeted attacks, into the Great London Sewer. The narrative is told through the medium of sketchbooks, produced by the Old Man of this lost community surviving in no-man's land.

George Thomson, The Sound Stage, Iver, Buckinghamshire, 2018
Artwork from the final scene of the film. The area of Farlows Lake, Iver, was eventually flooded, submerging the Sound Stage. The structure thus becomes a forgotten remnant of the lost community of the Great London Sewer.

STAGE

JG Ballard's short story 'The Sound-Sweep'[1] provided a starting point rather than a narrative framework for the Sound Stage project, which is located within a future vision of the M25 after a series of attacks on the Bluewater shopping centre – a notion suggested by Ballard himself – now known as the Great London Sewer. The notion of collection is borrowed from the Ballard text; however, it now has an architectural implication, as artifacts washed up from the sewer are used in the construction of the community infrastructure and eventually the creation of a performance space: the Sound Stage. The project is based on a sketchbook (itself fictitious) retrieved from the ruins of the community and drawn by the central character, the Old Man.

The project exists beyond this proposed future and imagines an excavation of what the community was like, illustrated in film to create an animated version of the sketchbook, describing the development of the community and its eventual failure within the no-man's-land of the Great London Sewer.

The community abandoned the old M25 motorway after the attacks; protection, they decided, came with a perimeter fence, a no-mans-land, border zone, a gateway. The M25 was once the connection to London; now, its defensive barrier.

The Old Man had been living out of his car before the attacks, washing in the toilets of the Clacket Lane services; now he remained in this abandoned monument to the old road. No one maintained the zone. Cracks filled with weeds spread across the road surface, as water rose from beneath. The blind paranoia that created the zone calmed in the ensuing years, and the community decided to reclaim it. The old infrastructure was beyond repair, so they proceeded with the plan for the Great London Sewer.

Artwork from the film indicating the Sound Stage afloat the Great London Sewer. The film provided an animated version of the drawings from the fictitious sketchbook of the lost community.

Artwork from the film showing the amphitheatre in front of the Sound Stage.

The Old Man was not a labourer before the attacks, but decided to enlist in the sewer construction. A life in the uncertainty beyond the walls was better than the controlled existence within them. After construction the Old Man, and the growing community of zone inhabitants, surveyed the empty landscape, searched for possibilities in the wilderness, and collected waste brought by the sewer current and items from the ruined road.

The community settled in Farlows Lake near the parish of Iver, once a popular fishing spot, which had high stocks of big catch, eels, pike and perch that swam among the shopping trolleys and traffic cones. The floating market was built directly on the lake from metal carcasses salvaged from the old road. The adjacent plots of land were cleared of rubble and used to grow stunted vegetables.

The community was built and run on collected items. Scaffolding, clamps, cones and road signs could all be used in its construction. The prize find was a gramophone, a forgotten object. The wind-up mechanism was a revelation. This was a community beyond the infrastructure of the domestic city: no gas fires, no light switches, no electricity. With only one record it was decided that a large structure was to be built to replicate the gramophone. The large horn would play the vibrations of water, ripples of sewage replacing the grooves of vinyl. Vibration and movement were inherent to the floating existence of the community. Performances were held in the vast amphitheatre below the horn, a notion that had been lost in the paranoid and oppressive existence within the London walls. The Sound Stage, as it was known, was the community centre, a cathedral built on the tenets of collection, performance and mobility.

The community had sustained life in the zone, and word of the Sound Stage spread beyond the city walls. Its performances, events, the spectacle, reminded the dwellers within the walls of what they had lost.

Gradually rising rainfalls and breaches in the sewer wall completely flooded Farlows Lake and the surrounding area of the zone. The Sound Stage had been abandoned long ago, after sanctions forbidding public gatherings spread to encompass the zone. Perhaps somewhere on the concrete bed of the flooded motorway, a part of the Sound Stage remains. Now, this cathedral of performance, which had offered a different way, lies drowned as another monument to the derelict motorway, a relic of what could have been. **ↁ**

Note
1. JG Ballard, 'The Sound-Sweep' [1960], in *The Complete Short Stories: Volume 1*, Harper Perennial (London), 2006.

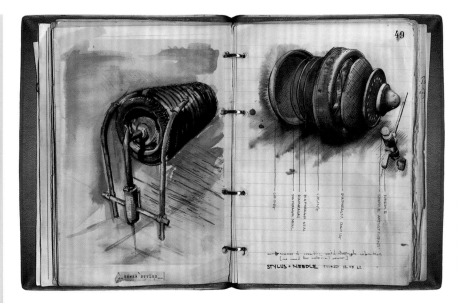

Extract from the found sketchbook of the Old Man, indicating his sketch design for the sewer stylus, a means of playing the vibrations of the sewer current, amplified by the Sound Stage.

Extract from the sketchbook showing Farlows Lake market, constructed from the detritus washed up by the sewer current and from the remnants of the Great London Sewer's previous incarnation as the M25 motorway.

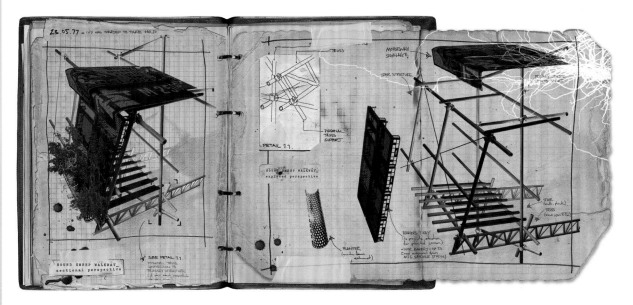

Extract from the sketchbook indicating the detail of the Sound Stage's perimeter staircase. This would have served as a construction drawing within the community.

Recent History – Art In Ruins

Some two decades on, guest-editor **Nic Clear** returns to the work of Hannah Vowles and Glyn Banks of collaborative art practice Art in Ruins. As cited by Brian Hatton on their behalf in 1989: 'in the city of the future everything will be historical (ie visited) for fifteen minutes'.

It seems appropriate to end this issue on the near future with a series of works from the near past that predicted a type of future that we now experience as the present.

In the 1980s, at the height of postmodern Post-Modernism[1] and before the world had heard of the term 'young British art', Art in Ruins made a series of gloriously provocative works and installations utilising the fragments of the culture around them, celebrating the death of art – or was it the art of death? Their work was a perfect condensation of Jean Baudrillard's term 'Game with Vestiges',[2] but unlike Baudrillard, rather than giving up on art as a spent force, they continued to pursue the critical potential of art practice even as art became more and more allied with the entertainment industry.

Art in Ruins is a partnership between an artist and an architect. They have steadfastly refused to acknowledge disciplinary boundaries; art and architecture are just labels placed on 'closed systems'. If the system is open then the labels do not matter.

The name Art in Ruins is itself wordplay. Is the state of art ruinous or are they making art among the ruins, or both? It is a name that links them to both nihilism and romanticism, although there is always something romantic about nihilism.

While their work was self-consciously decorative, it was also unsettling and awkward; it looked like one should be able to simply swallow it whole, but was a conceptual pill covered in sugar that concealed far more difficult and complex issues. If everything is equivalent, how do we attach values to anything? In a system of mass production, what status does the artist have as a site of authenticity? Where do the lines implied in the simple binary oppositions of good taste versus bad taste, or high culture versus low culture, actually start and finish?

Like everything by Art in Ruins, the contribution to this issue is carefully worked out and thought through; in many ways it is a continuation of their earlier practice with 'fragments' from their own 'history' collected and displayed as museum pieces.

Art in Ruins were never solely about image. The nature of the two texts they have chosen for this issue, one from a review and the other one of their own 'text pieces', play with the idea of the site of a text as a crucial element in the construction of its meaning; and when these texts are shorn of their original context (the design newspaper and the gallery wall) they function as ambiguous signifiers and ask us to consider how should we read them. In doing this, words are treated in the same sense as the objects shown in the photographs of their installations. Are we looking at these elements for their own individual value and meaning? Or should we consider the totality of the assemblage as a single work?

Contemporary museum practice tends towards a simplification and banalisation of art through the myth of transparency; art should be democratic, open to everyone, simple and understandable. Art in Ruins suggest that even when the signifiers are simple and everyday, the signification can be more abstract and difficulty should not be seen as a problem.

Art in Ruins have declared themselves 'in limbo' and I hope this does not last for too much longer. One hope for the near future is that we witness their return to active production – the world needs Art in Ruins.

Notes
1. Postmodernism is a critical term developed by Frederic Jameson to describe the cultural logic of late capitalism. Post-Modernism is an uncritical term developed by Charles Jencks, literally meaning after Modernism. For a full account of this lexical minefield, see Dick Hebdige, 'Staking Out The Posts', in *Hiding in the Light*, Comedia (London), 1988, pp 181–207.
2. Jean Baudrillard, 'Interview: Game with Vestiges', *On the Beach 5*, Winter 1984, pp 19–25.

Art in Ruins, *Drawing from Cities of the Dead: New Realism – From the Museum of Ruined Intentions*, Gimpel Fils Gallery, London, 1987.

Art in Ruins, *Drawing from Cities of the Dead: Grand Opera*, Bonner Kunstverein, Germany, 1988.

In our wonderful culture, everyday life has become nothing more than a form of window shopping. As we wander (as Baudelaire's flâneur) as detached and aristocratic 'free individuals' from object to object (fragment to fragment) through the Cities of the Dead of our great museum of ruined intentions searching for signs of life, we are at the same time afraid that our sentimental attachments may turn into Fatal Attractions ('Liaisons Dangereuses').

When attitudes become sales we live a life of ruins in the new realism of our Postmodern social condition where we buy time as tourists in our cultural supermarket, awaiting the 'catastrophe' which will liberate us from the twilight zone of corporate bodies and designer subjectivities.

Art in Ruins, *Sans Frontieres* Text Work, 1984–2001

Art in Ruins, *Drawing from Cities of the Dead: Vampire Value*, École des Beaux Arts, Tourcoing, France, 1988.

The notion that art arises from the heightened sensitivity of peculiar individuals is a romantic notion; most art of all times has been collective. In the 20th century, projects to revive collective art have mostly been connected with totalitarianism, but Warhol matured in the very peculiar collective, or mass (the two words are virtually interchangeable despite capitalist claims to the contrary) society that has come to be known as 'consumerist'. This society allows a high degree of apparent individual freedom, but at the cost on the one hand to communal identification and on the other to any enduring or transcendent meaning to the individualism that it encourages. This was aptly summed up in Warhol's adage 'In the future, everyone will be famous for fifteen minutes'.

... Acquisition and tourism are versions of each other, even substitutes for each other, rather as kitsch and avant-garde both symptomatise a global placelessness. ... In the work of Art in Ruins avant-garde art and architecture, as well as uplifting monuments and prestige technology, are implicated in a general entropy of significant value. ... The effect is more tendentious and allegorical than Warhol, but that is possibly because Art in Ruins seem more interested in history than fame, and more interested in the end of public meaning in 'tourism' than the end of the individual subject in 'stardom'. 'In the city of the future' they might say, 'everything will be historical (ie visited) for fifteen minutes'. Δ

Extracts from Brian Hatton, 'Secret Destiny', *Building Design*, No 957, October 1989, pp 42, 44

Contributors

Michael Aling studied at the Bartlett School of Architecture, University College London. He has worked for Bohn&Viljoen and Matthew Springett Architects, and is currently a design tutor at UCA Canterbury and the University of Brighton. He is a film-maker in his spare time.

The Art in Ruins collaborative art practice was founded in 1984 by **Glyn Banks and Hannah Vowles**. They have exhibited and been published internationally, curated exhibitions, written for the art and architecture press, lectured in schools of art and architecture, and at conferences and symposia. They were awarded the DAAD stipendium of the Berliner Künstlerprogramm and were guest professors at the Munich Academy of Fine Art. Art in Ruins has been in limbo since 2001. Hannah Vowles is Senior Academic at Birmingham School of Architecture

John Culmer Bell founded FXV, a studio concerned with researching the potential of new technologies and media in design, in 1999. He has exhibited and lectured widely in the UK and internationally. After a period at the Arts Council of England, he joined the Architectural Association as a unit master from 2000 to 2006. He is currently teaching at the Canterbury School of Architecture where he has developed the MA Digital Ekistics: the architecture and urbanism of online environments.

Richard Bevan studied undergraduate architecture at the Edinburgh College of Art and has worked on various projects for Gross Max Landscape Architects. He completed his postgraduate diploma in Unit 15 at the Bartlett School of Architecture in 2009, researching sonic spatial formations through time-based film media. He is a founding member of Seed Records, a London-based cross-genre record label and event-management organisation, and is also one half of the electronic musique concrète duo Posthuman. (www.seedrecords.co.uk).

Nic Clear is a qualified architect who teaches at the Bartlett School of Architecture and University for the Creative Arts Canterbury. He ran his own company, Clear Space, for many years before setting up the now defunct General Lighting and Power whose work covered everything from architecture to pop promos, and from advertising campaigns to art installations. He spends the rest of his time writing fiction and making drawings and films.

Dan Farmer graduated with Distinction from the Bartlett School of Architecture in June 2008. Since then he has spent time tutoring and acting as a guest critic for a number of universities, including the Bartlett School of Architecture, UCL, the Architectural Association, and the Universities of Nottingham and Canterbury. He spent four years working for Make Architects before leaving to complete his Masters in architecture, and now uses film, animation and motion graphics to generate and explore new architectural and spatial possibilities.

Matthew Gandy is Professor of Geography at University College London and Director of the UCL Urban Laboratory. His publications include *Concrete and Clay: Reworking Nature in New York City* (MIT Press, 2002). He has also published articles in the *New Left Review* and *International Journal of Urban and Regional Research*. He is currently writing a book on cultural histories of urban infrastructure.

Bastian Glassner is part of the award-winning trio of directors LynnFox. Founded soon after members Christian McKenzie, Patrick Chen and Bastian Glassner graduated from studying architecture at the UCL in 2001, LynnFox has since become a household name within the world of music videos and commercials. Firmly driven by a fascination with all things weird and wonderful, their collective work has attracted a vast array of clients and has been extensively screened around the globe.

David Greene is a founder member of Archigram. He was awarded, with Peter Cook, the Annie Spink Award for Excellence in Architectural Education in 2002. With a nervous, twitchy career from designing T-shirts for Paul Smith to freelance practical speculations for developers to conceptual speculations for Archigram and this article, he finds himself obsessed with the potential effects of new situated technologies on the room and in the garden.

Samantha Hardingham is an architectural writer and researcher. Publications include several books on the work of Cedric Price and a recent book on the work of David Greene, *L.A.W.u.N Projects#19* (AA Publications, 2008) accompanied by an exhibition at the Architectural Association, 'L.A.W.u.N Project #20: – Imperfect Works'. Samantha is a research fellow at the Centre for Experimental Practice, EXP, University of Westminster, a researcher at the Invisible University and a tutor in the First Year Studio at the Architectural Association.

Geoff Manaugh is the author of BLDGBLOG (http://bldgblog.blogspot.com/), an award-winning website launched in 2004, and of *The BLDGBLOG Book* (Chronicle Books, 2009). Bruce Sterling has called him 'the world's greatest living practitioner of "architecture fiction"', and according to *Icon* magazine he is one of the 50 'most influential architects, designers, and thinkers' in the field today. He is a contributing editor to *Wired* and *Dwell* magazines.

Ben Marzys obtained his diploma in architecture from the Bartlett School of Architecture. While at the Bartlett, several short films he produced there, including *London After the Rain*, gained international recognition through selection by OneDotZero, the London Festival of Architecture 2008, the Bloom competition organised by OneDotZero and MTV, and the Canary Wharf Film Festival. He has recently moved from London to Brussels to join the Lab[au] team.

Ben Nicholson was educated at the AA, Cooper Union and Cranbrook Academy, and teaches architecture at the School of the Art Institute, Chicago. He lives and works in New Harmony, Indiana. His publications include *Appliance House* (MIT Press, 1990) and a satire *The World Who Wants It?* (Black Dog Publishing, 2004). He has exhibited at the Canadian Center of Architecture, the Cartier Foundation, the Whitney Museum and the Venice Biennale. He is currently writing *Horror Vacuii*, which reveals number, geometry and labyrinths through beans, sand drawing and walking, and also a book about Frederick Kiesler, while continuing work on micro-infrastructural design projects in New Harmony.

Laurent-Paul Robert and Dr Vesna Petresin Robert of Rubedo explore transdisciplinary methods integrating visual arts, design, film and sound using customised digital tools. Their work has been shown at the Cannes Film Festival, Beijing Architecture Biennial, Royal Academy of Arts, Royal Festival Hall and the Venice Art Biennale. Rubedo is based in London where Laurent has also created visual effects for award-winning films and Vesna currently teaches at the Bartlett and Central Saint Martins.

Simon Sellars is a freelance writer and editor based in Melbourne, Australia. He publishes the website Ballardian (http://www.ballardian.com), and in March 2009 he was awarded a Doctor of Philosophy from Monash University for his thesis '"The yes or no of the borderzone": JG Ballard's Affirmative Dystopias'. He continues to be inspired by everything from the topography of cereal boxes to the anthropology of non-place urban fields.

Soki So is an Australian Chinese from Hong Kong, currently based in London. He studied architecture at the University of Hong Kong before receiving a graduate diploma at Unit 15 from the Bartlett School of Architecture in 2008. His interest in film and architecture lies in the generation and extension of space through the inhabitation at phenomenal, experiential and operational levels.

George Thomson completed his undergraduate degree in architecture at Edinburgh University, before joining Unit 15 at the Bartlett, UCL. He worked for two years at Heatherwick Studio in London and Hong Kong, and currently works as a freelance illustrator for Formation Architects. He has a small design office, I.N.K, working on private projects including the Gighouse (Glasgow, Scotland), which is currently under construction.

+ CONTENTS

Snøhetta

It is not unusual for a practice to take off after winning a major competition. But Snøhetta was founded to enter one. **Jayne Merkel** explains that the Oslo-based firm flourished almost immediately after winning the international competition to design the Alexandria Library in Egypt in 1989. Ten years later, a victory in a blind international competition for the New National Opera in their home city paved the way for Snøhetta's practice today, which is largely devoted to cultural centres. And although the democratic lifestyle of the office is distinctly Scandinavian, the architects and designers who work there and the projects they work on now span the globe. There is even a New York office in the heart of Wall Street.

The name of this practice reveals its character. Snøhetta is named not after the partners, but after a distinctly peaked mountain in northern Norway. The firm stands out for exquisite, thoughtful public work that grows out of its landscape context. Lecturing at the Architectural League of New York last autumn, the best-known principal, Craig Dykers, began by showing a picture of the group posed class-picture style in their amphitheatre-like concrete loft on a fjord in Oslo. 'Our office is very diverse,' he said. 'If someone else was standing here, he or she might present us very differently.'

Dykers went on to explain that 50 per cent of the hundred people who work at the firm are male and 50 per cent are female. Seventy per cent are architects, 15 per cent landscape architects and 15 per cent concentrate on interiors. 'The staff is internally unionised. All entry-level people make $65,000, and principals $113,000. There are two open work areas and no private offices. We have five weeks' paid vacation, 10 national holidays, and we try not to work beyond 5, 6 or 7pm.'

When this writer visited the New York office in the grand old Cunard Steamship Lines Building overlooking the big bronze bull of Wall Street, all the workstations were empty because everyone was in a meeting. Afterwards, Dykers explained that it is not always easy to be democratic, but he looked relaxed, and nobody seemed unhappy as he wandered back to his desk.

Most of the New York-based architects are working on the Memorial Pavilion for the nearby World Trade Center site, a library at the University of North Carolina for the Institute for Emerging Issues, a 1,300-seat theatre and creative arts school for Virginia Tech University, a collaborative art school for Bowling Green State University in Ohio, or a Music Hall at Queens University in Kingston in Ontario, Canada.

Clearly, Snøhetta's early success in competitions for a major library and concert hall led to the work they have gone on to do, though they also have commercial projects now.

The New York office in the Cunard Building in Manhattan. The 20 or so architects in the New York office occupy a mezzanine level space with views of the big bronze bull of Wall Street out of the window facing Broadway, and also of the very grand classical interior spaces of the building once occupied by the Cunard Steamship Lines. Here, Craig Dykers leads a meeting in an open work area.

Snøhetta architects and designers in the Snøhetta office, an old concrete industrial warehouse on a fjord overlooking the harbour in Oslo's Vippetangen district. There are no private offices and profits are equitably distributed between the architects, landscape architects and interior architects around the world.

King Abdulaziz Center for Knowledge and Culture, Dhahran, Saudi Arabia, due for completion in 2012
This sleek, modern, almost extraterrestrial-looking structure with a tubular stainless-steel skin rises out of the smooth barren desert landscape with bulbous forms that resemble gigantic seeds, beans or ancient

King Abdulaziz Center for Knowledge and Culture, Dhahran, Saudi Arabia, due for completion in 2012
The $300-million cultural centre, financed by the Aramco Oil Company, is intended to preserve Saudi history and introduce international modern culture to Saudi society with an archive, museum, exhibition hall, library, lifelong learning centre, children's museum, auditorium, a cinema, cafés and restaurants.

In 1989, Dykers was living in Los Angeles where he had won some competitions that had not materialised. Kjetil Trædal Thorsen and Øyvind Mo were living in Oslo, where they had formed a collaborative studio with a group of landscape architects upstairs from a beer hall named Dovrehallen after the mountain range where Snøhetta is the highest peak. Dykers, Thorsen and their Austrian friend Christoph Kapeller, who was also living in LA, were all interested in entering the Alexandria Library competition, so they formed a team – and ended up winning. Dykers and Kapeller then moved to Norway where Snøhetta as we know it was born, and the Norwegian government helped them get established and negotiate contracts for the library. Today, Dykers and Thorsen are the principals; the partners are architects Ole Gustavsen, Tarald Lundevall and Robert Greenwood, and landscape architect Jenny Osuldsen.

The impetus for the Alexandria Library competition went back to a time in the 1970s when US president Richard Nixon visited Egypt and was asked what he would like to see. 'The pyramids and the Alexandria Library,' he replied, causing some embarrassment to his hosts who had to explain that the library as a place had not existed for several thousand years. Before too long,

the US donated money to begin planning to rebuild the library and create an electric grid capable of sustaining it. Then UNESCO took over the project. In 1988, the UIA (International Union of Architects) helped plan a competition. By 1990, $65 million had been raised, mostly from the Arab states, to begin design and construction.

'While we were working on the library, which opened in 2002, the Berlin Wall came down and the September 11th attacks took place,' Dykers noted, so the meaning of the library and its importance changed significantly.

The new $220-million Bibliotheca Alexandrina occupies a site near that of its ancient predecessor, between the university and the harbour. The most distinguishing features of the 7,432-square-metre (80,000-square-foot) structure are a curved wall of grey Aswan granite and a round, sloping 32-metre (105-foot) high glass-panelled roof, tilted towards the sea like a sundial. Measuring 160 metres (525 feet) in diameter, it creates a fifth facade for the 96,277-cubic-metre (3.4-million-cubic-foot) reading room on 11 cascading levels that is the largest in the world. The complex also houses a conference centre, specialised libraries for the blind, young people and children, three museums, four art galleries, a planetarium and a manuscript restoration laboratory. Since there is no modern building industry in Alexandria, much of the work was done by hand. The complex was inaugurated on 16 October 2002.

Bibliotheca Alexandrina, Alexandria Harbour, Egypt, 2002
The Alexandria Library contains the largest reading room in the
world, with 70,000 square metres (229,659 square feet) of space
on 11 levels. It will hold eight million books as well as the meeting
spaces for scholars that its ancient predecessor contained.

Although Snøhetta did a few other projects while the Alexandria project was under way – a school, a fishing museum in Karmøy, Norway, and the Norwegian Embassy in Berlin – the practice was cemented by its victory in competition for Oslo's New National Opera in 1999. This building, too, has a waterfront site, as many of Snøhetta's buildings do, and it is also made of stone, in this case La Facciata, an Italian marble that is self-supporting, has the proper acoustic properties and comes from a country with a great operatic tradition. The white marble is used here in a way that recalls the Norwegian landscape, which is rugged and often cold, hard and dry. Marble slabs form a folded ground plane that seems to rise out of the sea, and zig and zag in various directions, covering the box-like, aluminium-clad 'factory' to the rear where the production facilities are located, and rising up on the harbour side to reveal glass walls up to 4.5 metres (15 feet) high around the main auditorium and various lobby spaces. The glass walls, reinforced with glass fins for stiffness, are made of low-iron glass to make them as transparent as possible.

Though it looks very solid, the New National Opera is built on an infill site where a sawmill stood for 150 years, in an area now being redeveloped. Reviving it, the architects reintroduced the natural

Bibliotheca Alexandrina, Alexandria Harbour, Egypt, 2002
above: The Alexandria Library occupies a space between the university and the harbour, near where the ancient library was located. The circular form of the tilted roof of the reading room echoes the shape of the nearby harbour.
left: This great curved granite exterior wall surrounds the reading room. Like much of the building, it was carved by hand. It is inscribed with characters from 120 different scripts, so it both symbolises and embodies the purpose of the library. It is made of granite from the same Aswan quarry that supplied the temples at Karnak.

New National Opera, Oslo Harbour, Oslo, Norway, 2008
above: The stage curtain in the traditional horseshoe-shaped main concert hall was created by Los Angeles artist Pae White with images of aluminium foil transferred to a computer-driven loom. Walls and balconies are sheathed with oak.
opposite bottom: The building is covered with a 'carpet' – an angular mountaintop-like marble roof – that extends to the edge of the sea, creating a public gathering place. After the opening in 2008, 28,000 people came to stroll across it and celebrate the new building even though many had not come to see a performance.

landscape into the valley. Though the competition called for a monument, Snøhetta created 'a building you look past rather than at', with a 'carpet' on top – a mountain-like marble roof that extends to the water's edge where swans have reappeared in the newly clean water.

The structure contains a horseshoe-shaped, 1,400-seat concert hall surrounded by a curving oak 'wave wall' which is visible on the exterior, a 400-seat theatre for dance and various contemporary arts, and a 150-seat experimental 'black box' theatre which doubles as a rehearsal room. There is a bistro, a café with a view of the harbour, a generous multistorey lobby as well as a back-of-the-house 'highway' and private grassy garden for the 650 people who work there. Artists, some chosen through competitions, collaborated on various aspects of the design. The Danish artist Olafur Eliasson designed the white, perforated, illuminated cladding that surrounds the bathrooms. The random pattern in the oak wall, which enhances acoustics, was created by children with learning difficulties.

The sense that architecture is not just made to serve society, but to uplift it, prevails in the King Abdulaziz Center for Knowledge and Culture in Saudi Arabia, a $300-million cultural centre with an archive, museum, exhibition hall, library, lifelong learning centre,

left: The oak-panelled, 1,400-seat main concert hall for operatic and symphonic performances is surrounded by tiers of curved balconies designed to enhance visibility and acoustics.

below: The curving oak 'wave wall' which surrounds the concert hall is visible from the outside through curtain walls, which are reinforced with glass fins and made of low-iron glass to enhance their transparency. The generous multistorey lobby is supported by columns that tilt because the beams and piles, which anchor them under water, are not aligned.

children's museum, auditorium, cinema, cafés and restaurants that will be open to both sexes. Women will be permitted to drive in the surrounding area. Funded by Aramco Oil, the centre is clearly intended to provide alternatives to the very traditional fundamentalist institutions elsewhere in the country. The 65,000-square-metre (699,654-square-foot) building itself resembles a precarious stack of gigantic metal beans or metallic dolmen set end to end, vertically – a fitting image for a daring cultural venture. The facade is composed of an externally ventilated double wall system. The outside wall, which acts as a rain- and sunscreen, is made of stainless-steel tubing wrapped around the building volumes with the pipes squashed over the windows to allow views out and still provide shading. The windows themselves and a climate wall comprise the inner layer.

Located in Dhahran, in the Eastern Province, the institution's intention is to preserve Saudi history and promote new cultural development within the region. Snøhetta was selected in a limited competition which Zaha Hadid and Rem Koolhaas also entered. A 1,000-seat auditorium will be used for opera, symphony, musicals and lectures. Below ground, the museum and archive surround an inner void that represents beliefs and knowledge found within the kingdom of Saudi Arabia. Above ground, the composition reaches out to the world beyond its borders both physically and symbolically.

Ironically, perhaps, Snøhetta is also designing the Memorial Pavilion at the World Trade Center site, the only visible building in that complex. In 2004, the practice was selected to design two museums – a branch of the non-profit Drawing Center, which had long been located in SoHo, and a new International Freedom Center. However, plans for both institutions were abandoned when political tensions erupted between families of victims and other constituencies vying for control of the site. It was eventually decided to have only a memorial park with rectangular pools where the towers once stood and an underground memorial museum (being designed by Davis Brody Bond), but Snøhetta was retained to build the one new freestanding structure located there. The sleek but quiet, metal and glass-clad polygonal building, which ranges in height from 17 to 22 metres (57 to 72 feet), will serve as a meeting place and entrance to the underground museum and house a 180-seat auditorium, a private room for relatives of 9/11 victims and a small café, as well as various security screening devices and mechanical services for the museum and nearby transit hub. The structure will also contain two pairs of the distinctive Gothic-arched columns salvaged from Minoru Yamasaki's World Trade Center towers.

No particular formal quality unifies Snøhetta's growing body of work. Every building is unique; though their forms derive from their sites, they do so somewhat differently in each case. Yet every one of the buildings has a certain quiet poignancy that makes its existence seem not just important but essential. Δ+

World Trade Center Memorial Pavilion, New York, 2004–
above: The $80-million metal-and-glass pavilion will be the only above-ground structure on the memorial site. It will be located between the quiet pools marking the positions of the World Trade Center towers and will serve as a beacon for the area at night.
opposite: The metal-clad polygonal pavilion will be the entrance to the site's underground museum as well as a meeting place for victims' families and other visitors. It will also house mechanical equipment for the surrounding area.

Text © 2009 John Wiley & Sons Ltd. Images: pp 98, 100 © MIR; pp 99, 105(b) © Snøhetta; pp 101-2, 104, 105(tr) © Snøhetta, photos Gerald Zugmann; p 103 © James Willis; p 105(tl) © Nicolas Buisson; pp 106-7 © Visualisation by Squared Design Lab, courtesy of the National September 11 Memorial & Museum

Biochemistry Department, University of Oxford

Howard Watson describes how Hawkins\Brown's new Biochemistry Department for the University of Oxford represents an innovative new model for scientific research institutes. Spatially, its interior not only positively embraces and encourages social interaction and the fertilisation of ideas, but also brings art, architecture and science together under a single roof.

Oxford's new Biochemistry Department takes the lessons of the most progressive and creative work environments into the usually secretive, insular, closed lab world of scientific research. This works counter to the usual stereotype of the white-coated scientist furtively hiding away in his lifetime pursuit of an ultrapersonal mission. Here, the building and especially its interior architecture are seen as paramount to the fertilisation of ideas.

London-based Hawkins\Brown was brought in to create a £49 million, 12,000-square-metre (129,166-square-foot) building which reappraises the way in which scientists can work together. The firm has established a good reputation within the educational field, particularly for further education and university establishments, and is currently undertaking impressive new designs for Kingston and Coventry universities. It is also furthering a keen understanding of the possibilities of cultural architecture through the Nottingham New Art Exchange and the ongoing 'civic hub' of the Corby Cube.

The latter buildings may express a desire to transmute ideas from 'inside' to 'outside' – to fracture the established closed set of performer/audience relationships in order to bring diversity – but the design of the Biochemistry Department marks a new departure for the practice. It is about using architectural design to make practitioners communicate and thereby open up new possibilities: to add new factors to the equation; to provide the heat to ignite solitary elements into adventurous new compounds.

Hawkins\Brown, Biochemistry Department, University of Oxford, 2009
above: The exterior features multicoloured glass fins and artist Nicky Hirst's *Glass Menagerie* design, inspired by the Rorschach inkblot test, which provide both decoration and opaqueness for the new home of sensitive scientific research. Oxford has strict building-height restrictions, so the four storeys are augmented by two more below ground, lit by a large light shaft and eight rectangular skylights.
opposite: Art and communication drive the design, with the informal communal areas of the atrium dressed with artworks inspired by scientific research. Annie Cattrell's huge sculpture, *0 to 10,000,000,* hangs down the central space of the atrium.

The ground-floor café, the only publicly accessible area of the building, has a laboratorial cleanliness, leavened by beech ceiling panels and splashes of colour on the chair backs. Morag Morrison of Hawkins\Brown describes the variety of seven chair backs as 'like a scatter of pills'. The café overlooks the atrium through the frames of Nicky Hirst's *Portal* artwork.

Despite their educational work, Hawkins\Brown feel they were appointed because they came to the idea of the research department without preconceived notions. They have not even consciously drawn upon any of the more radical new research buildings at American universities or Will Alsop's 2005 Queen Mary Institute of Cell and Molecular Science in London. Rather, their inspiration came from analysing the existing research department and the way the scientists work. The result has been a simple realisation of a series of functional skins from the outside to the central atrium: laboratory service corridors, laboratories, write-up areas and, finally, the core atrium.

Usually, one would expect the greatest permeability for a progressive new building to be expressed by the exterior skin, with the architects and clients charmed by the siren call for accessibility. Not here. The labs need light, but they also require great privacy. Consequently,

the mostly glazed exterior plays a game of conceal and reveal, with multicoloured glass fins and an artwork by Nicky Hirst, based on the Rorschach inkblot test, placed on to the glazing to create a 60 per cent opaque surface which also cuts down solar gain. The main entrance to the building is virtually hidden among the large panes of glass and, apart from the ground-floor café, visitors cannot advance beyond the small reception area without authorisation. The permeability grows as the skins proceed inwards, with the open-plan lab write-up areas bleeding into the atrium without barriers and the central core itself working as the social heart of the building.

The 400-square-metre (4,305-square-foot), six-storey atrium is a delight of interior architecture, radically fulfilling the client's desire to increase interaction and communication – to get the array of internationally esteemed geniuses to exchange ideas and blur the boundaries of their science. Clad in beech veneer, the atrium has great warmth by contrast to the brightly lit labs. The idea of linking, with obvious parallels in molecular formation, is made immediately apparent through a series of suspended staircases and walkways,

above and right: The theme of encouraging the scientists out of their labs into a central core of exchange is further emphasised in the lab write-up areas, which are open-plan extensions of the atrium.
top: View upwards to the ceiling of the beech-clad atrium, with linked stairways and walkways bridging the volume and highlighting the theme of connectivity.

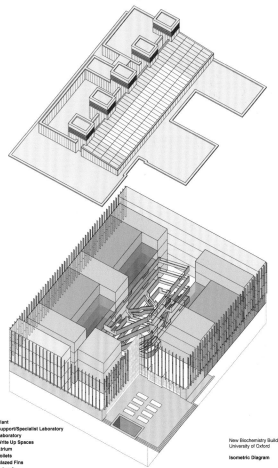

Plant
Support/Specialist Laboratory
Laboratory
Write Up Spaces
Atrium
Toilets
Glazed Fins
Artwork

New Biochemistry Building
University of Oxford

Isometric Diagram

Isometric view of the design showing the complex atrium in the core of the building.

somewhat jokingly inspired by Harry Potter's Hogwarts, which fly across the atrium, their linearity fractured by midway resting points. These resting points are intentional, aimed at providing further places for exchange and communication. The result is angular, and it is hard to perceive the overall order as the various sections traverse space, as if the minds of the scientists are finding new pathways of logic.

The atrium is surrounded by 'break-out' places, including a green roof terrace, pockets of hard chairs and tables, and areas of upholstered furnishings, particularly on the lower ground floor, featuring Nigel Coates' curving Hitch Milius Oxo seating system along with HM20L tables. Like the staircases and wooden cladding, throughout the interior there are humorous radicalisations of ancient educational motifs, particularly those of the surrounding Oxford colleges. Rather than stiff-backed or leather club chairs, here the furniture is informal, the chairs' curved sides fitting into each other for intimate arrangements. On the lower ground floor, the old-school Turkish carpet has become a radical artwork. Designed by artist Tim Head and resulting from a residency in the Structural Bioinformatics and Computational Biochemistry Department, the digitally printed carpet, called 'Open Field', creates an apparently random but repeated pattern inspired by the way scientists try to express visualisations of their research.

The link between art, architecture and science is key to the design intention of establishing a creative, thought-provoking environment. According to Morag Morrison, Associate Director of Hawkins\Brown and leader of the interiors team: 'Initially the scientists were nervous. We took them to the William Dunn School of Pathology in Oxford, where photographic artist Catherine Yass had a residency, and that inspired them. In the end we found that the scientists were very, very creative people. Working with the artists gave them confidence in the process.'

The initial budget for artistic commissions was a mere £15,000, but blossomed as the scientists came to understand art's central role in the building's new purpose. Called Salt Bridges, the site-specific art project was led by Nicky Hirst, who helped strengthen the ideas of playing with collegiate conventions and the relationship between scientific and artistic creativity. As well as her inkblot work, she has inscribed the misted-glaze corner overlooking the atrium from the café with an ornate picture frame inspired by the symbols that biochemists use. Annie Cattrell, meanwhile, has evolved the idea of the classical chandelier in a sculpture made up of 150 twisting bird-forms that hang down from the atrium roof, inspired by the similarities of the movements of flocks of starlings and the fluidity of particles in plasma.

The architectural success of the Biochemistry Department is already beginning to be acknowledged – the building has won a 2009 RIBA regional award. But, more importantly, applications to work in the department have doubled as scientists have immediately recognised the benefits of the stimulating environment. Ð+

Howard Watson is an author, journalist and editor based in London. He is co-author, with Eleanor Curtis, of the new 2nd edition of *Fashion Retail* (Wiley-Academy, 2007), £34.99. See www.wiley.com. Previous books include *The Design Mix: Bars, Cocktails and Style* (2006) and *Hotel Revolution: 21st-Century Hotel Design* (2005), both also published by Wiley-Academy.

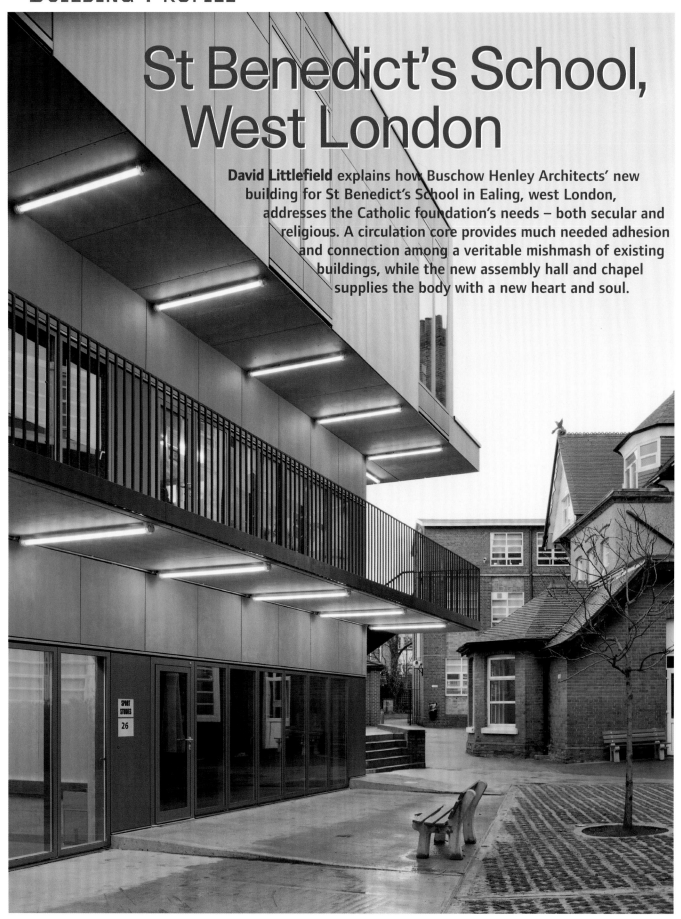

St Benedict's School, West London

David Littlefield explains how Buschow Henley Architects' new building for St Benedict's School in Ealing, west London, addresses the Catholic foundation's needs – both secular and religious. A circulation core provides much needed adhesion and connection among a veritable mishmash of existing buildings, while the new assembly hall and chapel supplies the body with a new heart and soul.

Buschow Henley Architects have a reputation for delivering fine-tuned buildings. Their projects are multi-layered, in the sense that meaning, reference or plain old association is considered at the front end of design. Director Simon Henley certainly enjoys talking about his work, and his presentations typically cover the deeper, narrative-based agenda of a building, letting the actual physical form (which can speak for itself) go somewhat undescribed. So what could the practice make of the jumble of uncoordinated spaces that made up St Benedict's School in Ealing, west London? How could these architects salvage anything remotely meaningful from a context that was untidy at best – at worst, botched?

The practice have done this sort of thing before, though – their project for TV company TalkBack (2002) is a good example of how to slip a certain reverence for space and ritual into a very practical building. They have now reprised this achievement at St Benedict's. The school, established by Benedictine monks a little over a century ago in the residential suburb of Ealing, needed

help. Over its lifetime it had accumulated an eclectic range of buildings, dating from the 1890s, the 1930s, the 1960s and the 1990s; no new development had much of a relationship with what had preceded it (the brick monolith of a decade ago is ridiculously lumpen and faceless). The brief to the architects was merely a list of spatial requirements, but Henley saw what was really needed – a soul, a sense of purpose and institutional gravitas.

'They asked us: can you build us two halls, one for exams, one for assemblies; a language lab; music rooms; a chapel; a new entrance; new loos; a sick bay ... all sorts of stuff,' remembers Henley, who saw two possible solutions. The first was an entirely new block, separate from the cluster of other buildings, which could provide everything asked for while being limited by its own terms of reference; option two was to drop something into the centre of the pre-existing buildings, tying them together and providing a certain critical mass to an otherwise dispersed and fragmented place. Henley chose this latter option, partly because the creation of a stand-alone building would have replicated the problems of the campus, and partly because it was 'more interesting'.

Buschow Henley Architects, St Benedict's School, Ealing, London, 2008
above: Classrooms in the new building tend to be square in plan, typically 7 x 7 metres (23 x 23 feet). This is to enable a variety of teaching styles (teaching can be done from the centre, for example) while the format provides better views of smart boards.
opposite: The new three-storey classroom wing provides one side of a new plaza. The school contains an eclectic range of architecture. Although Buschow Henley added a new language to the mix, their building makes spatial sense of the others.

The coffered concrete ceiling of the central hall. Light is admitted from above. The new chapel, which sits atop this large space, acts as a flue for the natural ventilation strategy.

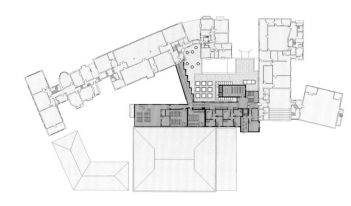

Second-floor plan. The building rises in a series of three main steps, the last stage of which is shown here. The chapel is seen as a rectangular box, joined to the rest of the development at one corner.

The requirement for two halls was the key. Buschow Henley's solution was to give the school just one. But they have been clever about it. The exam hall was to have been of around 225 square metres (2,422 square feet), while the assembly space needed to be much larger at 400 square metres (4,305 square feet). What the practice has done is to drop one into the other, a 15 x 15 metre (49 x 49 foot) square within a 20 x 20 metre (65 x 65 foot) square. Large doors ring the inner hall, allowing it to be sealed off, but when opened the generous circulation spaces beyond bleed into the centre to create that larger assembly hall. This is the new heart of the school. Placed in the centre of the older buildings, and nestling up against them, the new hybrid space is the fulcrum around which the ebb and flow of school life runs; it is, in effect, the circulation core, but one of such proportion, rhythm and generosity that staff and students are still learning how to use it. 'It's a pure, idealised space around which everything happens. It's a void, but it's a very useful void,' says Henley.

The large space, with its coffered ceiling and regimented lines of doors, is reminiscent of a cloister surrounded by smaller spaces. In fact, the new entrance to the school is very small indeed – a single-storey box with projecting fins that seem to welcome visitors with outstretched arms, gathering them in. Through this little vestibule is a neat and sensible reception room, through which is discovered Henley's 'void'. These spaces are therefore deliberately graduated on a rising scale of small, bigger, biggest, much like that encountered in a carefully modulated church; Buschow Henley withhold their bold statement until you are well inside the building. This is not the private-sector Catholic equivalent of the government's new city academies where visitors are greeted by office-like atria and glass

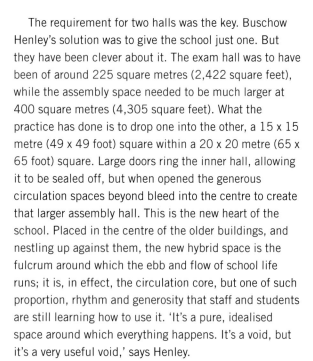

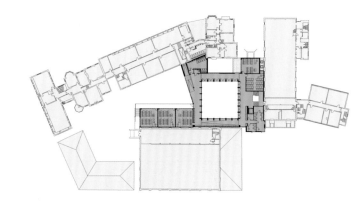

First-floor plan. Classrooms spin off from the centre like a set of armatures. Ramps make connections with the floor plates of neighbouring buildings.

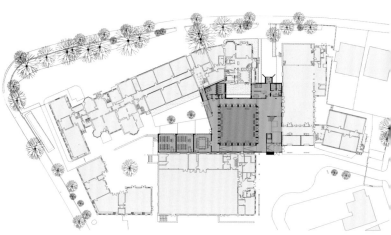

Ground-floor plan. The inner hall provides the centre of gravity, around which everything pivots. The entrance appears at the top of the coloured image.

top: The rooftop chapel, seen as the grey box, left of centre.
Viewed from outside, the chapel gives away little or none of its
true purpose, appearing instead like a piece of machinery.
bottom: The central hall at St Benedict's, with full-height doors
open to show the spaces beyond. When the doors are open,
the 225-square-metre (2,422-square-foot) examination hall can
become a 400-square-metre (4,305-square-foot) assembly hall.

top: View into the central hall. When functioning as an examination hall, the doors at ground and first-floor level are closed.

above: Section through the development showing the 1990s gymnasium on the left and a late 19th-century house on the right. The new development sits between these buildings.

right: Buschow Henley's project at St Benedict's involved linking the surrounding buildings, built in different periods. The building provides the central circulation core, as well as halls and classrooms.

canopies; St Benedict's manages to achieve something quieter but no less dramatic. Black-swathed Benedictine monks do not look out of place here.

Perched atop the inner hall – off-centre, sharing the rooftop with glazing units that illuminate the space below – is the chapel. This little boxy structure, of engineered timber rather than the concrete much in evidence elsewhere, is the equal of the clever and cavernous space beneath. The careful placing of glazed slots in the facade, along with the deep narrow beams of the roof structure, contrive to fashion a series of Christian crosses without overdoing it; in fact, one might be forgiven for missing the reference entirely. What makes this little chapel more potent is that it is entirely unexpected. It is a discrete enclave that draws back from the hubbub of school life, while its external appearance (seen from a corridor which wraps the periphery of the roof) is more M&E facility than place of worship. Indeed, the chapel does act as a flue for the natural ventilation strategy at work in the halls.

In plan, this building is very much an infill structure. Probably half of its edges press up against the buildings which surround it (permanently obscuring one length of the 1990s gymnasium). But it does not fill the entire space available – an inner courtyard is left empty, from which the brick walls of an early building can be seen, while a trapezium-shaped plaza is created between the strip of new classrooms and a well-mannered block from the 1930s. Classrooms, incidentally, tend to be square in plan rather than rectangular, to provide more flexible spaces for teaching practice and offering better views of smart boards. Something else the building does rather well is negotiate the changes in levels across the site, linking up different floor plates through gentle ramps.

As a school building, this development is unique – not because of its responses to the peculiar constraints of the site, but because of the determination to create something unashamedly institutional and a little awe-inspiring. ⅅ+

David Littlefield is an architectural writer. He has written and edited a number of books, including *Architectural Voices: Listening to Old Buildings* (2007) and *Liverpool One: Remaking a City Centre* (2009), both published by John Wiley & Sons Ltd. He was also the curator of the exhibition 'Unseen Hands: 100 Years of Structural Engineering', which ran at the Victoria & Albert Museum in 2008. He is a visiting lecturer at the University of the West of England.

Migration Pattern Process

Within the international community architects are regularly typecast as exporters of predetermined solutions, rarely given the opportunity to respond appropriately, sensitively and effectively to specific and real emergencies. At the core of any impact are people like you and me; their welfare and successful healing creates a catalyst for the community to rebuild lives and esteem. Since 2007, Diploma Unit 7 at the Architectural Association in London, led by **Simon Beames and Kenneth Fraser,** has been researching the philosophical, social, political, economic and technical response to long-term humanitarian relief and the resocialisation of displaced people and damaged communities in conditions of extreme hardship.

Asif Khan and Julia King (AA Diploma Unit 7), One Year House, Mae La refugee camp, Thai/Burmese border, May 2007
As part of a unique mapping exercise, Khan and King hired a plane to gain an accurate description of the settlement along the dangerous border.

Time lapse view of the prototype construction at the Mae La refugee camp. Local craftsmen adapted the students' proposal and the two groups collaborated to construct a single-family house for performance assessment.

above: A patch of silicon jointing, designed with the ambition of improving house construction in the area. The work spans five operative scales from bamboo connections to strategies for settlement orientation and distribution, tested on site through a 1:1 house prototype.
left: Proposal for intervention and improved durability of self-build houses at the Mae La camp showing members of the community load-testing the proposed fixing components.

Any programme responding to human situations requires fluidity. Although there is a five-year plan in place for research in Diploma Unit 7, it has to adapt so that fieldwork is appropriate and accessible for the unit's members. Research must be undertaken and completed within a single academic year, but its impact must also extend far beyond that for the participants. Students must be prepared to develop an operational network, established initially by a unit brief and introductions to key sites, experts and communities; this is then supported through the academic year by philanthropic engineers, architects, philosophers and economists.

It is a fact of humanitarian work that adaptability, humility and the ability to listen and interpret others must be combined with technical capability and design method. Students have to develop their own relationships and ultimately provide real communities with an insight into the possibilities of architectural intervention, but at all times they must not forget the reality of each situation and the fact that what they can offer, as students, is limited.

Before engaging at ground level, exhaustive research culminates in a design handbook. This collective research is intended to help appropriate the effort and allow only productive time on the ground, where sites are found, researched and analysed, and students penetrate the culture and return with a degree of empathy and vision for engagement.

Political Migration, Burma, 2006–07

Mae Sot in Thailand, on the Burmese border, has a large population of displaced people fleeing the oppressive military regime in Burma. Students were asked to participate in this context as architectural researchers, where economics, political and social components, materiality and constructability were given equal priority. Students Asif Khan and Julia King answered these questions with direct action.

Having secured funding from the British Council and won the RIBA McAslan Bursary, Khan and King established a relationship with the Thai Burma Border Consortium. This enabled them to develop a component-driven approach to housing within the 90,000 person Mae La refugee camp. Due to climate and limited resources the existing self-built houses have a very short life expectancy, which is considerably less than the occupancy of their displaced and persecuted inhabitants; within a single annual cycle houses rot from the root and collapse from the corners.

King and Khan engaged with local craftsmen and collaboratively developed a new prototype house, using transference of technology to reduce the quantities of bamboo, protecting the structure with a 'dry sock' termite-resistant footing, and also to repel mosquitoes through ceiling adaptations. These innovations were tested on site through the building of a 1:1 house prototype. Assessment of its performance is ongoing, and the concept of temporary has begun to be challenged in a situation where society has been denied permanence.

Environmental Migration, Bangladesh 2007–08

The Ganges delta, in Burma's neighbouring state of Bangladesh, is home to 100 million. It has the most densely packed human population on earth. Climatic extremes range from near desert to swamp forests, together with monsoon floods and cyclones. Communities survive through tactical short-term 'environmental' migration.

The original research plan was to investigate the flood-prone region; however, two weeks before the intended visit Cyclone Sidr hit the delta. The unit was invited by BRAC, the country's largest NGO and effective bank and government, to provide detailed research into the potential relief of people suffering in the aftermath of this event.

Students adapted immediately and developed a fluent understanding of the region's rural communities; hence, the year's programme continued the development from component to shelter. Each investigated resolutions in increasing scale, assembling an argument based on the critical evaluation of available material systems with the transference of developed economy technologies. Millions of bricks are manufactured in Bangladesh, and although they are an ideal construction resource, they are a more valuable economic asset when exported. Several students used sophisticated engineering principles currently unavailable to rural communities to design efficient, high-performing structures using a limited quantity of bricks, thus protecting incomes while creating homes.

Working with a research group including technologists and theorists responsible for live field projects, Bonnie Chu identified a unique opportunity. Through her determined investigations and skilful networking in the UK and Bangladesh, she formed a working relationship with International Red Crescent that enabled her to research the building of an emergency shelter for women. Following her graduation, she has been able to consolidate this work through the chance to spend a further year's research in the field.

Economic Migration, Ethiopia 2008–09

The locus of global poverty is moving to cities, a process now recognised as the 'urbanisation of poverty'.
United Nations Human Settlements Programme, *The Challenge of Slums: Global Report on Human Settlements*, 2003[1]

An extension of the previous two years' work has been the research into typologies of model towns. This was taken to a territorial level in the Lalibela region of northern Ethiopia. Collaboration with research partners aimed at an implementable master plan that would promote micro-

Johnny Gao (AA Diploma Unit 7), Deployable Cinema, Lalibela, Ethiopia, 2008
A crowd gathers around the students' Deployable Cinema on the first night of the short film festival.

George Woodrow (AA Diploma Unit 7), Deployable Cinema, Lalibela, Ethiopia, 2008
The Deployable Cinema spirals out across the only flat site in Lalibela, making use of the natural amphitheatre to provide maximum viewing opportunities for the local community.

Students assembled a fabric structure in Lalibela, having transported the entire assembly required for the cinema from London.

opposite: As part of the consultation process in Ethiopia, students from the AA engaged the local community to build a cinema in which to host a short film festival.

enterprises while addressing a development's social needs within the context of post-famine trauma, drought, poverty and aid reliance. Students were expected to propose interventions that were technical, social and critical with a particular emphasis on the development of systems that are capable of development and construction.

A prototypical, portable and deployable structure accompanied the unit to Lalibela. This structure was managed economically and transported by the group along with all the equipment for a self-sufficient cinema, presenting a five-night film festival during the visit. While the excitement of the audience of children, beguiled by the strange object and intrigued by the images that flickered on the screen under the stars, was reward enough, there was a wider significance to this effort. A tool for engaging with the community at all levels, the cinema enabled students to obtain rare insights into this unknown place, resulting in 12 individual proposals that together now form a master plan for Lalibela. A new approach to the complex wider issues of development and long-term aid dependence, these projects are influenced by first-hand field experience.

The unit attempts to equip students operating within extraordinary, often traumatic contexts, but essentially expects individual engagement with self-sought situations. Since 2007, certain issues have remained constant despite the world's great geopolitical and cultural diversity. Appropriate application of technology and energy is essential, but is disregarded as being imperialistic unless implemented through complete community interaction. Strategies tested through extensive research and development will be accepted by the most disengaged authorities when economic advantages are made evident.

There is clear evidence of successful knowledge transfer, the development of systems based on a local technological context, renewable resources and hybridity, which is now resonating through the students' work in developed economies. Δ+

Simon Beames is a director of Youmeheshe (youmeheshe.com) and architect for COTE, an NGO involved in construction and resocialisation following conflict and disaster, working on community projects in Romania and Kosova. Previously at Grimshaw, he led projects including the redevelopment of Battersea Power Station. He has taught at the Architectural Association since 2003.

Kenneth Fraser is a principal of Kirkland Fraser Moor Architects (http://k-f-m.com). Previously at Renzo Piano Building Workshop, he was project leader for the Rome Auditorium and the Padre Pio Pilgrimage Church. He has taught at the Architectural Association since 2006.

'Unit Factor' is edited by Michael Weinstock, who is Academic Head and Master of Technical Studies at the Architectural Association School of Architecture in London. He is co-guest-editor with Michael Hensel and Achim Menges of the *Emergence: Morphogenetic Design Strategies* (May 2004) and *Techniques and Technologies in Morphogenetic Design* (March 2006) issues of *Architectural Design*. He is currently writing a book on the architecture of emergence for John Wiley & Sons Ltd.

Note
1. United Nations Human Settlements Programme, *The Challenge of Slums: Global Report on Human Settlements*, UN-Habitat, 2003. From the foreword to the report by United Nations Secretary-General Kofi Annan, p v.

Mathematics of the Ideal Pavilion

Neil Spiller flees the nihilism of the shards and blobs of the last three decades in architecture and finds redemption on the north shore of Lakeside Way in Kielder Water, Northumbria. He describes how with this exquisitely tailored pavilion sixteen*(makers) are opening the way for a new way of working.

In the 1980s, when the architectural profession entered its nihilist phase (when it recognised that God or reason and certainly morality were no longer influencing architecture), a lot of disjointed, shard-like spaces were posited. These errant geometries were little more than illustrations that vistas, orthogonality and often commodious proportion were a thing of the past, a defunct affectation of an old order.

Much of this nihilism has continued in a new guise: the double-curved banana, the gherkin, the spiced doughnut or, indeed, the gilded parsnip, have replaced the shard. Plans are all about slipping and sliding from one unpredictable social situation to another to exchange ideas and cultures for the benefit of one's corporate sponsor. Sections seem to be devoid of structural rationale and kinky.

The mantra goes that as long as we can draw our building, our computers and our engineer can make it. This is all well and good as long as we stay in the realms of cyberspace. But the moment we transverse the outer limits of virtuality and blip into reality we are confronted by things architects used to be taught about, such as 'bending moments', Young's Modulus, the 'radius of bending' and 'span to depth ratios'. These among a myriad of reality's little games conspire against architects who have been too seduced by the computer's ethereal muse.

Not so sixteen*(makers), who have just made, not just designed, a most beautiful pavilion known as Shelter 55/02, situated on the north shore of Lakeside Way in Kielder Water, Northumbria. The interesting thing about it, apart from its appearance, is that the finished piece was evolved by the process of its making and there are no finished drawings. Designed in collaboration with sixteen*(makers)' siblings

sixteen*(makers), Shelter 55/02, Kielder Water, Northumbria, 2009
Canopy detail.

Sliding screen under construction.

View looking
southeast over
Cock Stoor.

View from the
southeast corner,
near to completion.

Stahlbogen GmbH, Shelter 55/02 was 'grown' from the hybridised digital and analogue fabrication techniques they have spent the better part of 20 years perfecting. Its form or detail is never a compromise as a way of mediating between idealised drawing and lumpen reality because this binary opposition is never set out in the process.

The little structure is the antithesis of Rem Koolhaas' notions of architectural surrender embodied in his ideas for 'Bigness'. 'Bigness is impersonal: the architect is no longer condemned to stardom … Beyond signature, Bigness means surrender to technologies; to engineers, contractors, manufacturers, to politics, to others. It promises architecture a kind of post-heroic status – a realignment with neutrality.'[1] This is an architecture born out of technical design knowledge, knowledge of materiality, of jointing and of exquisite architectural tailoring.

Let us just take a few sentences to explore its aesthetic. Like certain politicians it has something of the night about it, a tad Batman and a tad Stealth. Equally, it gives the impression that a maverick sheet-piler

supported by Boeing has just lucked out. This is not just a fabrication soufflé; its form is deeply related to its context, and in this way it is picturesquely set in its landscape, responding to views and vistas and framing details. Thus on one level it plays Miesian games of varying degrees of enclosure, and on another the landscape itself becomes the experiential glue that holds it together. The scheme is a tidy little ying and yang between the natural and the artificial.

One hopes to see many more building-sized propositions from sixteen*(makers); the architectural pendulum seems to be swinging in their direction. I like it because it is different. Difference is the key to the vitality of our profession – and no one mentioned 'parametrics' while it was being made. Δ+

Neil Spiller is Professor of Architecture and Digital Theory and Vice Dean at the Bartlett, University College London.

Note
1. Rem Koolhaas, 'Bigness: The Problem of Large', *S,M,L,XL*, Monacelli Press (New York), 1995, pp 513–14

Computational Building Performance Modelling and Ecodesign

Khee Poh Lam and Ken Yeang call for architects to play a more proactive role in building performance modelling. They look at how this is all made possible with the emergence of accessible, cost-effective web-based systems for practices and the way that this can further be enhanced by integrated performance-based design approaches.

Advancements in building performance simulation over the past two decades have been significant, with new and improved computational tools that address the changing needs of ecodesign throughout the building delivery lifecycle – from design concept generation to detailed design, construction, commissioning and even building operations and controls.

The ultimate goal of these computational developments is to support ecodesign and the creation of healthy, comfortable and productive habitats for human activities. Ironically, defining such human activities 'accurately' as input factors in performance modelling remains probably the single most complex and challenging task. For example, research has shown that for a variety of reasons (such as dynamic work schedules and modes of operation), actual occupancy rate in modern office buildings is frequently only 40 to 60 per cent of the design assumption. This has consequences not only on energy consumption but also on the maintenance of comfort conditions in buildings. Mismatch between designed and actual operating conditions results in excessive provision of heating/cooling and difficulty in optimising control of building systems.

This challenge lies squarely with the architect, whose responsibility is to thoroughly understand the client's operational requirements and translate this 'qualitative' descriptive brief into an architectural design solution, accompanied by appropriate quantitative parameters that can be communicated to the engineering design team members for producing concurrent technical solutions.

Recognising a critical role of communicating building performances, especially during early design stages, should prompt architects to play a more proactive leadership role in building performance modelling. Simulation tools continue to evolve to address, among others, two major objectives: firstly to make simulation tools more accessible to the architectural profession, and secondly to enable effective 'real-time' sharing of design information between the entire project design team.

Accessibility entails offering cost-effective, ubiquitous (web-based) simulation services to the architects/engineers especially in the early design phase. Green Building Studio (GBS)[1] is one such example. The service provides quick preliminary energy prediction, based on the architect's design (represented by an object-oriented CAD model) and specifying two basic input parameters: building type and geographical location. Based on these, the service derives a set of assumed building specifications (construction type, mechanical system and so on), from its increasingly rich database of buildings in various cities in the US. It then uses the well-known DOE-2 energy-simulation engine to generate the results. In addition, GBS also provides the input file that can be used for further detailed design application and analysis by engineers.

Underlying this simulation service is the essential capability of connecting the CAD (geometric) model and the energy computation model. Such data 'interoperability' has been the focus of organisations such as the International Alliance for Interoperability (IAI)[2] and the Green Building XML Schema.[3] While their implementation strategy may differ (for example, top-down versus bottom-up), their missions are similar: to define and publish specifications

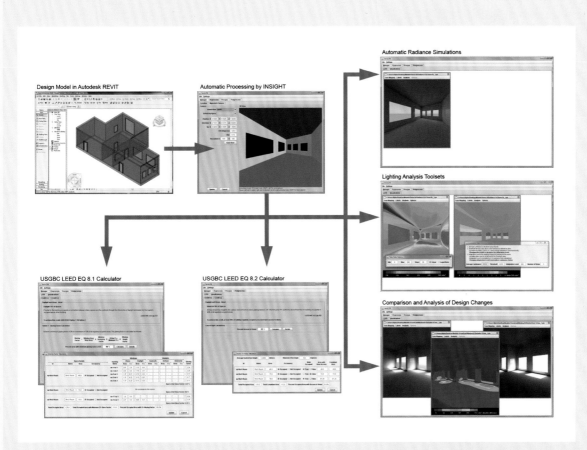

YC Huang and KP Lam, Features of the new INSIGHT lighting simulation tool, 2009.

(schemas) for building information modelling (BIM) as a basis for sharing building information globally throughout a project lifecycle, across professional disciplines and computational design-support applications.

The quest for sustainable and green developments has led to the increasing adoption of integrated performance-based (as opposed to the conventional discrete prescriptive-based) design approaches. New and more stringent building performance targets such as higher energy efficiency standards are emerging internationally from both developed as well as developing countries. Some standards have become regulatory requirements while others remain voluntary benchmarks. The Leadership in Energy and Environmental Design (LEED) Green Building Rating System is an example of the latter – a nationally accepted benchmark for the design, construction and operation of high-performance green buildings in the US. Since its inception in 2001, 2,799 projects have been LEED certified and more than 20,000 have been registered for certification. Major public agencies and private corporations in the US have adopted policies mandating LEED rating for newbuild and retrofit projects.

The teaching and R&D pursuits at the Center for Building Performance and Diagnostics (CBPD) at Carnegie Mellon University have been contributing to the advancement of simulation tool development and application. For many years, a course on building performance modelling has been offered to graduate and senior undergraduate students from both architectural and engineering backgrounds. This provides valuable experience in learning across disciplines, and gaining the practical working knowledge of simulation tools in energy, lighting, airflow, integrated systems and control, and so on that is increasingly in demand in the industry.

In the research realm, besides exploring new theories in computational design support systems to meet changing needs in an information technology world, efforts are deployed to create 'seamless' and 'intelligent' interfaces between CAD and performance simulation engines. For instance, in relation to the LEED rating system, Jerry Yudelson in '"The Change Function" and Green Buildings' observed that: 'Those in a position to determine the future of LEED should continue to reflect on how to make it more transparent and user-friendly to those in the trenches of building design, construction and operations.'[4] The CBPD has recently completed a research project entitled 'Integrated Concurrent Design of High Efficiency Commercial Buildings', sponsored by the National Institute of Standards and Technology (NIST) Advanced Technology Program and United Technologies Corporation. The project includes the creation of a 'seamless' interface between the REVIT CAD model and the Radiance Lighting Simulation engine to support early design exploration in lighting performance. The tool imports a REVIT model and, based on the specified building type and location, the necessary Radiance input files are generated and populated with 'appropriately assumed' relevant building input data (where data is missing) for the project. Furthermore, the tool also automatically analyses the building's spatial configuration as well as the lighting results to determine whether the design fulfils the requirements of the LEED Indoor Environmental Quality (EQ) Credit 81 (daylight for 75 per cent of spaces) and Credit 8.2 (views for 90 per cent of spaces).

The World Business Council for Sustainable Development recently published its first report on energy efficiency in buildings, which states that buildings are responsible for at least 40 per cent of energy use in

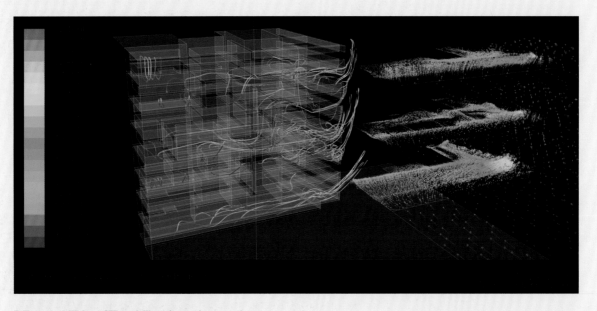

R Zhang and KP Lam, CFD modelling of natural ventilation in a multistorey office building showing velocity pathlines and distributions, 2009.

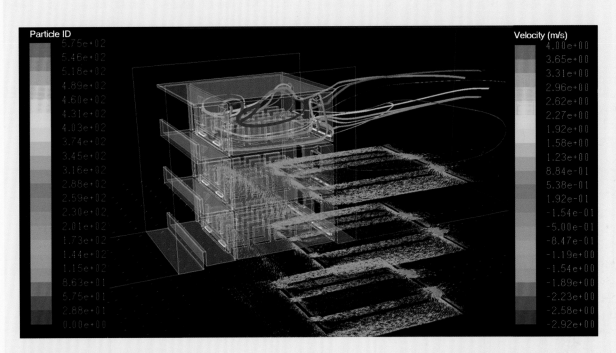

Particle ID

| |
5.75e+02
5.46e+02
5.18e+02
4.89e+02
4.60e+02
4.31e+02
4.03e+02
3.74e+02
3.45e+02
3.16e+02
2.88e+02
2.59e+02
2.30e+02
2.01e+02
1.73e+02
1.44e+02
1.15e+02
8.63e+01
5.75e+01
2.88e+01
0.00e+00

Velocity (m/s)

4.00e+00
3.65e+00
3.31e+00
2.96e+00
2.62e+00
2.27e+00
1.92e+00
1.58e+00
1.23e+00
8.84e-01
5.38e-01
1.92e-01
-1.54e-01
-5.00e-01
-8.47e-01
-1.19e+00
-1.54e+00
-1.89e+00
-2.23e+00
-2.58e+00
-2.92e+00

R Zhang and KP Lam, CFD modelling of natural ventilation in a school building showing particle flow pathlines and velocity distributions, 2009.

many countries, mostly by consuming energy derived from fossil fuels.[5] Energy use is increasing by an annual rate of more than 3 per cent in the US alone, and is growing rapidly in countries such as China and India. Worldwide energy consumption by buildings is expected to grow by 45 per cent over the next 20 years.

The concern is not just about the sustainability issues related to dependency on non-renewable sources of energy, but is equally, if not more importantly, about the impact of byproducts of energy production systems on the environment and their effects on climate change. The building industry is being challenged to create energy-efficient and high-performance buildings and this starts right at the project inception, when the client meets the architect for the first time to formulate the design brief. As can be seen, cost-effective and sophisticated (but user-friendly) tools are constantly being developed and offered to the multidisciplinary design team to concurrently support these complex simulation tasks. A new generation of designers is being trained with knowledge of these tools and their application in real-world conditions. Δ+

Professor Khee Poh Lam, Professor of Achitecture at Carnegie Mellon University, teaches architectural design, building performance modelling, building controls and diagnostics as well as acoustics and lighting. His fields of research are in total building performance (TBP) studies and the development of computational design support systems. He currently serves on the board of editors of the *Journal of Building Performance Simulation* and *Building Simulation: An International Journal*. He is also a building performance consultant on several award-winning projects and is a member of the Energy Foundation board of directors.

Ken Yeang is a director of Llewelyn Davies Yeang in London and TR Hamzah & Yeang, its sister company, in Kuala Lumpur, Malaysia. He is the author of many articles and books on sustainable design, including *Ecodesign: A Manual for Ecological Design* (Wiley-Academy, 2006).

Notes

1. See www.greenbuildingstudio.com/gbsinc/gbs-web.aspx.
2. See www.iai-na.org/about/mission.php.
3. See www.gbxml.org/about.htm.
4. See www.igreenbuild.com/cd_2503.aspx.
5. World Business Council for Sustainable Development, July 2008. The full report can be found at www.wbcsd.org/Plugins/DocSearch/details.asp?DocTypeId=25&ObjectId=MzE0Njg&URLBack=%2Ftemplates%2FTemplateWBCSD5%2Flayout%2Easp%3Ftype%3Dp%26MenuId%3DMTE2Nw%26doOpen%3D1%26ClickMenu%3DLeftMenu. A copy can be downloaded from www.wbcsd.org/DocRoot/nPf1MZCxRjSVFOdomMAE/WBCSD_EEB_final.pdf.

McLean's Nuggets

Topologically Speaking

In *Mathematics*, David Bergamini's excellent popular science survey of the subject, he includes a chapter entitled 'Topology: The Mathematics of Distortion'. Quoting the anecdotal testimony of fellow mathematicians he writes that a topologist is a mathematician 'who does not know the difference between a ring-bun and a coffee cup'.[1] Meaning that 'topologically speaking', these geometric figures are the same and with the right kind of material (perhaps not dough or fired clay), one can be transformed into the other. Both the bun and coffee cup have a genus of 1, meaning that they have one hole in each or, more precisely, that one complete cut can be made across the hole that does not divide the object into two. In the case of a solid sphere, a single complete cut anywhere on a sphere will divide it in two pieces, giving it a genus of 0.

Other noted topological curiosities include the Möbius strip, which has only one side and if cut in half longitudinally does not produce two loops, but a single larger two-sided strip. Stranger still is that if you attempt to cut a Möbius strip longitudinally into three equal widths, what you get is one long two-sided strip and a connected Möbius strip with its continuous side and single edge. A topological cousin of the Möbius strip is the zero-volume Klein bottle, which has only one surface and therefore no outside or inside; quite some skill is required to construct or 'blow' such remarkable Pyrex glass vessels. To view the world's largest Klein bottle, look up enigmatic astronomer and writer Clifford Stoll,[2] who now splits his time between stay-at-home-dad, the teaching of high-school mathematics and the making of Klein bottles.

If you think the Möbius experiments are not bad topological parlour tricks, then try removing your waistcoat[3] (I believe men wear them at weddings) without removing your jacket, which is perfectly possible and proves, 'topologically speaking', that it was never beneath your jacket in the first instance.

In a paper entitled 'Taxonomies of Form Based on Morphogenesis',[4] Professor John Frazer and Timothy Jachna investigate the usefulness of taxonomies used in generative product design. One of the criteria explored is the 'topology of relations between components' and how, by recording these topological interactions, the manufacture and assembly of man-made products could be improved. The example studied is the fabrication of writing instruments such as the ballpoint pen, although this design approach is eminently scaleable and as a process could be very useful in the future assembly of larger-scale architectures.

A diagrammatic sequence showing that it is indeed possible to remove a waistcoat without removing one's jacket.

Not Convenient

In the technological world of the public convenience, it appears that men have the best provision of impromptu de-watering holes. In a preventative move to discourage geographically random (antisocial) urination, certain local authorities in London have devised new relocatable (sometimes) 'pop-up' pissoirs, which in the case of the Urilift urinals[5] installed in Cambridge Circus and Villiers Street, Westminster, in 2002, literally rise up out of the ground. Between the hours of 7pm and 6am these mains-connected conveniences are deployed to prevent the diuretic properties of beer corroding any nearby landmarks. This rather neat piece of civic hydraulics could equally be utilised to raise any number of time-based utilities and services. Meanwhile, Hackney and Islington councils regularly provide temporary relief in the form of mobile urinals. Dropped off in 'wet areas' on Friday and Saturday nights, these moulded plastic cruciform units are capable of handling four 'customers' at a time and a total of 1,250 visits. This kind of provision is not new and the pissoir-style urinal in Regency Place, Pimlico, has long been a useful convenience for London taxi drivers who refer to its unique, if rather austere, architectural styling as the 'iron lung'. Incidentally, local authorities in the UK are prevented from charging money for the use of public urinals under the Public Health Act of 1936. If you have problems locating a suitable location for a 'comfort break', then look no further than www.thebathroomdiaries.com, a global directory of more than 12,000 public bathrooms, or wait for any number of phone applications for satellite-assisted locatable washrooms … Satlav anybody?

Deployment of the Urilift.

The Evolution of Thinking

If we accept for a moment Professor Steve Jones' recent assertion in an interview on the BBC Radio 4 'Today' programme[6] that human evolution has stopped or at least slowed to the point of imperceptibility, then we may enjoy his corollary and useful observation that 'we are the only animal that evolves in its mind compared to its body'. Jones' argument about the end of human evolution is that because of a decline in mutation and variation in the Western world, because of fewer old fathers (we start later, but finish early), there are less inherited differences and as a consequence 'all the components (of human evolution) seem to have lost much of their power'. This kind of 'grand averaging' has tended to make us more similar than different, and more genetically complex and resilient. Because of our evolving minds, Jones thinks this may save us from the potential catastrophic threats of a changing climate because we have invented our own climate: 'We take our climate with us, we all live in the tropics, even in the dire weather of today because we have clothes and central heating.' This tendency to technologically enhance our physical environs means that we increasingly obviate any need for any major human evolvement, although as Jones noted, human evolution takes place during huge periods of time; he described the 10,000 years since the beginning of farming (where, for instance, we evolved to digest milk) as a short interval of time in evolutionary terms, and ended the interview by reminding us that, 'If you are worried about what utopia is going to be like, you shouldn't be because you're living in it now'. ⌂+

'McLean's Nuggets' is an ongoing technical series inspired by Will McLean and Samantha Hardingham's enthusiasm for back issues of *AD*, as explicitly explored in Hardingham's *AD* issue *The 1970s is Here and Now* (March/April 2005).

Will McLean is joint coordinator of technical studies (with Pete Silver) in the Department of Architecture at the University of Westminster. He recently co-authored, also with Pete Silver, the book *Introduction to Architectural Technology* (Laurence King, 2008).

Notes
1. David Bergamini, *Mathematics*, Time-Life Books (New York), 1969, pp 159–60.
2. http://www.ted.com/index.php/talks/ clifford_stoll_on_everything.html.
3. Described as a 'vest' in the US.
4. Professor John Frazer and Timothy Jachna, 'Taxonomies of Form Based on Morphogenesis', Generative Art Conference, Politecnico di Milano University, Milan, 2004.
5. Urilift International, the Netherlands. See www.urilift.com.
6. See http://news.bbc.co.uk/today/hi/today/ newsid_7656000/7656220.stm.

Scaleable Technology for Smart Spaces

Living up to its name, Tinker.it! undertakes constructive fiddling. Valentina Croci describes how this Anglo-Italian practice is working in such a way as to open up new potential applications and to refine the user's experience. This has already been shown in work for the likes of Alfa Romeo and the museum at the University of Arizona Science Center, which is intended for permanent installation.

Tinker.it!, Alfa Romeo MiTo Totem, 2008
Together with LBI IconMedialab Milano, Tinker.it! created approximately 200 showroom totems for the launch of this new automobile. The totem contains a movement sensor that recognises the presence of the user and invites him or her to approach the device. During the stand-by phase a pulsing heart refers to the advertising slogan selected for the campaign: 'il cuore sportivo' (the sporting heart). A customised Arduino chip manages the entire system. The video software allows users to configure their own car, and the parameters of each selection generate a custom melody.

Tinker.it!, Scottie Bear prototype developed with the Waag Society, Amsterdam, 2007
This interactive toy allowed children recovering in hospital to communicate with one another. By manipulating the object on the special covering, it is possible to vary its colour and send tactile feedback to the other bear-receiver. Interactive technology thus allows for a mutation of the meaning and function of common objects and favours non-verbal forms of communication.

Interactive design continues to be an experimental discipline whose application is confined to temporary installations for events. As 'responsive' environments, these enable their intended audience to interact with them in more or less radical ways. Offering users a multi-modal experience, they immerse them in a context of images, sounds and tactile experiences, all of which are managed by complex systems. Rarely do we come across examples of interactive design that are part of a continuative corporate project: an investment in electronic and digital technologies that allows for an integrated and updatable series of user-oriented services, rather than a one-off interactive event/installation. This depends partially on corporate marketing's limited understanding of the potentials of new technologies and partially on the scarce compatibility between the hardware and software that is used. In general terms, any interactive installation or object is a one-off construction, and thus only on very rare occasions is it capable of dialoguing with other technological instruments. What is more, its contents are generally difficult to modify.

A step forward has been made by the group known as Tinker.it!, a nine-person company working between London and Milan, which was created in 2002 as a spin-off of the Interaction Design Institute of Ivrea. One of the group's founders, Massimo Banzi, is responsible for the design and production of the Arduino platform, in collaboration with another Ivrea-based company. The Arduino is an open-source microprocessor capable of developing interactive objects that can be autonomous or connected to common software – Flash, Processing and MaxMsp – or RFID radiofrequency technologies. Arduino chips can thus be connected to various types of output devices and sensors to create different user experiences.

Tinker.it! has also developed a series of modular elements over the years – touch sensors, joysticks or button-activated sensors – that represent a concise method of using interactive objects, even by those who are not experts in electronics. The group is also behind a software package known as Regista that is capable of controlling and overlapping the functions of the different software programs used for multimodal interactive works – for example, audio and video. Access to a platform of serial and modular devices allows for reductions in cost and time, as well as offering an increased compatibility between various devices.

If, as part of interaction design, we are beginning to apply hardware devices and software platforms in series, the attention of designers is now moving towards the electronic programming of the conceptual part of any project and, as a result, focusing on the dimension of the user's experience, opening up new possibilities that have yet to be fully explored.

Another characteristic of Tinker.it!'s work relates to the use of objects that many of us carry around in our pockets each day and which can be used to 'trigger' interactions; for example, the RFID-equipped Oyster card that can be used to activate software to modify the audio and visual effects of an installation. Other interactive interfaces often feature handles, arrows or buttons, rather than touchscreens, based on the consideration that the screens do not always offer the user clear affordance of manipulation, while physical and mechanical objects require more spontaneous gestures. What is more, touchscreens are rarely multiuser friendly in that they do not generally support the simultaneous interaction of more than one user.

Tinker.it!, Whirlpool stand, Milan Furniture Fair/Eurocucina, Milan, 2006
In collaboration with Syneo, a domestic space was here used to simulate the passing of one day in only 10 minutes. This smart space is a complex work of design that overlaps different scenarios and combines multimodal software with user-activated functions.

A number of home appliance prototypes were created and their user interfaces developed. The project thus represents an example of the coincidence between research and communication. The interactive elements included the spin cycle – a video of the washing machine activated by the user interface.

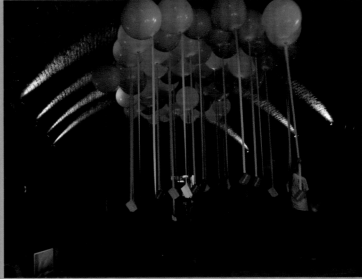

Tinker.it!, Workstation totems, YCN Award 08, London 2008
YNC (Young Creative Network), an agency that supports emerging creative talent, celebrated its annual award with an event showcasing the work of 90 young designers. Tinker.it! designed a series of workstation totems with handles that allowed users to choose and visualise the work of each artist. In addition, visitors were able to use their invitations, which contained RFID chips, to vote on and select their preferred works. The space also contained decorative balloons with flashing LEDs.

Looking at two examples of an updatable series of multimedia and interactive services, it becomes apparent how their work may extend beyond a single temporary event. Tinker.it! worked with LBI IconMedialab Milano on the launch of the new Alfa Romeo MiTo (2008), an automobile that offers a range of options for listening to music. Interactive totems were created for car showrooms with an interface that recalled the buttons on the car's radio. The totem provided access to a video program that could be used to create a personalised version of the car. By deciding on the variables of the layout, the software allowed for the composition of an exclusive melody, whose code could be sent by the user to the car dealer to transmit information about the selected options. The interactive video also offered access to the contents of a network of blogs written by Alfa Romeo aficionados alfisti and information developed by this online community. This enjoyable approach to developing brand loyalty also represents a hypothesis for more multimedia forms of communication.

A more complex project is that being developed for the University of Arizona Science Center. Here, Tinker.it! is working on a platform for creating interactive spaces based on a single system for hardware and software. The firm is designing not only a series of 'smart spaces' inside the museum — interactive and multimodal installations — but also a range of services to ensure that the user's experience of the museum does not end with a simple visit. For example, the project includes the use of the iPhone as a museum guide: less as a receiver of information and more as a tool to be used to select and customise the contents of a personal visit. Other possible functions include the possibility of 'book-marking' issues dealt with in the museum and using software to purchase additional information online. All of this is made possible by the use of a personalised RFID tag added to any cell phone to activate the different software operations. In this way, even the Web becomes an active part of a museum visit, allowing for the organisation of information about issues of interest. The design of interactive experiences is thus shifted towards a more participative form of use and a more complex series of services.

Developing such an articulated multimodal system is possible thanks to the use of hardware and software platforms designed as a group of single functions. The modularity of technology also allows for the revised design of smart environments in the field of retail. This means that in a chain of shops, for example, it is possible to implement economies of scale and simplify the maintenance of equipment as all use the same instruments. ⫢+

Translated from the Italian version into English by Paul David Blackmore.

Valentina Croci is a freelance journalist of industrial design and architecture. She graduated from Venice University of Architecture (IUAV), and attained an MSc in architectural history from the Bartlett School of Architecture, London. She achieved a PhD in industrial design sciences at the IUAV with a theoretical thesis on wearable digital technologies.

Architectural Design **Digital Cities** July/August 2009

What is Architectural Design?

Launched in 1930, *Architectural Design* is an influential and prestigious architectural publication. With an almost unrivalled reputation worldwide, it is consistently at the forefront of cultural thought and design.

Architectural Design is published bimonthly. Features include:

Main section
The main section of every issue functions as a book and is guest-edited by a leading international expert in the field.

Δ+
The Δ+ magazine section at the back of every issue includes ongoing series and regular columns.

Truly international in terms of the subjects covered and its contributors, *Architectural Design*:

- focuses on cutting-edge design
- combines the currency and topicality of a newsstand journal with the rigour and production qualities of a book
- is provocative and inspirational, inspiring theoretical, creative and technological advances
- questions the outcomes of technical innovations as well as the far-reaching social, cultural and environmental challenges that present themselves today

How to Subscribe

With 6 issues a year, you can subscribe to Δ (either print or online), or buy titles individually.

Subscribe today to receive 6 issues delivered direct to your door!

£198 / US$369   institutional subscription (combined print and online)

£180 / US$335   institutional subscription (print or online)

£110 / US$170   personal rate subscription (print only)

£70 / US$110   student rate subscription (print only)

To subscribe: Tel: +44 (0) 843 828
  Email: cs-journals@wiley.com

To purchase individual titles go to:
www.wiley.com